Why Me?

Help for Victims
Of
Child Sexual Abuse

(Even if they are adults now)

Fourth Edition

Why Me?

Help for Victims
Of
Child Sexual Abuse

(Even if they are adults now)

Fourth Edition

by

Dr. Lynn Daugherty

Cleanan Press, Inc.
Roswell, New Mexico

Why Me?
Help for Victims of Child Sexual Abuse
(Even if they are adults now). Fourth Edition

By Dr. Lynn Daugherty

Previous editions of this book were published in 1984 by Mother Courage Press, Racine, WI, USA; in 1986 by Boobook Publications, Balgowlah, NSW, Australia; and in 1987 by Ad. Donker, Rotterdam, The Netherlands.

ISBN 0-9771614-3-9

Published by:

CLEANAN PRESS, INC.
200 West First Street, Suite 323
Roswell, NM 88203

www.cleananpress.com

Table of Contents

Purpose of this Book
Warning—Disclaimer

Chapter One   11
Questions and answers
about child sexual abuse

Chapter Two   21
Understanding people
who sexually abuse children

Chapter Three   33
Stories from victims
of child sexual abuse

Chapter Four   55
The effects of child sexual
abuse on the victim
and the victim's family

Chapter Five   69
A guide to beginning recovery

Additional Resources
About the Author

Acknowledgements

The classification and descriptions of rapists and child molesters found in Chapter Two are based on the work of Nicholas Groth, Ph.D., and his colleagues. The concept of Child Sexual Abuse Accommodation Syndrome in Chapter Three is based on the work of Roland Summit, M.D. Some of the concepts and suggestions for recovery found in Chapter Four and Chapter Five come from the work of Suzanne Sgroi, M.D., and her colleagues.

Several people provided support and encouragement throughout this project. Larry Michelsohn, Esquire, assisted in a variety of ways, some of them legal. Abby Witt and Alice Duncan typed and typed and typed. My parents, Welden and Vivian Bayliss, encouraged me in this and all my endeavors. Barbara Lindquist and Mother Courage Press, publisher of the first edition of this book, turned it into the first bestseller for victims of child sexual abuse.

I thank all of these people, as well as the clients, both victims and abusers, who have shared their stories and their struggles with me. Their experiences and their efforts in therapy brought about the development of this book with the hope that it will help others like them reach their goals of leading happier, more productive lives.

Lynn B. Daugherty, Ph.D.

Purpose of this book

This book was written to be read by victims of child sexual abuse who are now teenagers or adults. It is also intended for counselors and others who want to understand and help these victims.

To the victim

The purpose of this book is to help you understand *what* happened to you and *why*. It is also meant to help you sort out your own thoughts, feelings and behaviors.

This book contains much factual information about child sexual abuse. It also contains stories told by other victims of child sexual abuse. They are retold to let you know that many children have suffered through experiences similar to yours. Many of these former victims have gone on to live happy, successful lives.

This book was written as a guide to help you recover from the negative effects of the abuse you suffered and to help you make a better life for yourself.

To the friend, relative or spouse of the victim

This book is intended to provide you with a better understanding of the experiences of victims of child sexual abuse. Just making an effort to understand a person's thoughts and feelings is sometimes the most helpful thing one person can do for another.

To the counselor

In addition to providing you with a better understanding of the experiences of victims of child sexual abuse, this book is designed as an aid to be used with victims in helping them recover from the negative effects of child sexual abuse.

Warning—Disclaimer

This book is not intended to replace the services of a professional mental health counselor, or to provide professional psychological services to you. If you need expert professional help, you should seek the services of a competent mental health professional.

Reading this book can bring back strong unpleasant thoughts and feelings. These could even lead to thoughts of suicide or other injury. If you find yourself overwhelmed by these thoughts or feelings, please seek professional mental health services immediately!

Every effort has been made to make this book as accurate as possible. However, there may be mistakes, both typographical and in content. Furthermore, this book contains information that is current only up to the date of publication. Therefore, this text should be used only as a general guide to understanding child sexual abuse and not as the ultimate source of information. Please learn as much as possible about child sexual abuse from all available sources and tailor the information to your own individual needs.

The author and Cleanan Press, Inc. shall have neither liability nor responsibility to any person or entity with respect to any loss or damage caused, or alleged to have been caused, directly or indirectly, by the information contained in this book.

Chapter One
Questions and answers about child sexual abuse

Here are some questions many people ask about child sexual abuse.

What is sexual abuse?

Sexual abuse takes place any time a person is tricked, trapped, forced or bribed into a sexual act. It most often involves unwanted touching of the victim.

Why is sexual abuse wrong?

Sexual abuse is wrong because it **hurts people**. Sometimes it hurts the victim physically. More often it causes the victim to suffer psychologically. It can cause mild to severe problems with fear, confusion, anger, shame, depression and lowered self-esteem for the victim. It can also cause other serious problems later in life.

Most people who were sexually abused as children go on to lead satisfying and productive lives, but many suffer from the effects of the abuse in some way, even years later.

Each person's body is special and belongs to that person alone. Each person has the right to decide who can touch his or her body, when it may be touched and how. Sexual abuse violates the right of each person to make important decisions about his or her own body.

What is the difference between sexual abuse and "normal sex play"?

It is normal for children to explore their own and other children's bodies. It is normal for children to touch their own bodies or those of other children in ways that feel good. This "normal sex play" is one way we learn about our bodies and our own likes and dislikes. It is also one way we learn about the bodies of other people.

Sexual abuse is different. It involves sexual activity that is tricked, trapped, forced or bribed. Usually one of the persons involved in the abuse is older, more knowledgeable, or more powerful than the other and takes advantage of this difference.

What happens during child sexual abuse?

Sexual abuse may include any type of sexual activity. It can range from forcible rape to gentle, but unwanted, touching. Being unwillingly exposed to sexual activity or the genitals of another or forced to show one's own genitals to someone else is also a form of sexual abuse. Abuse may occur "in person" or through images or written material, usually called pornography.

12

Who sexually abuses children?

Children are usually abused by someone older than themselves. Often the person is in some position of authority over the child. This may be an adult stranger, a parent or stepparent, an aunt or uncle, a grandfather or grandmother, a pastor or counselor, a teacher or an adult friend. It may be a teenage babysitter, an older cousin, an older brother or sister or an older child in the neighborhood. Eight out of ten child victims are sexually abused by someone they know and trust rather than by a stranger.

How does child sexual abuse happen?

Although violent sexual attacks of children sometimes take place, the sexual abuse of children usually involves more subtle force. This may be threats of harm or threats of "telling on" the child for some misdeed. Other times the child may be bribed with gifts or special privileges.

Children are often tricked into unwanted sexual contact. This may involve games, which start out as fun and end with unwanted contact. Sometimes the older person tricks the child by telling him or her that what they are doing is "OK" or that "everybody" does it, or that it is for the child's "own good."

The sexual abuser's power, knowledge and resources are greater than those of the child victim.

He or she exploits this difference to take advantage of the child.

What different patterns of child sexual abuse occur?

Child sexual abuse may be divided into three patterns. These patterns may have different effects on the victim.

Brief incidents

This type of sexual abuse may happen only once to a child. The abuser may be a stranger or an acquaintance. The abuse occurs as an isolated incident. A stranger may expose his genitals to a child who is walking down the street. An acquaintance may try to touch the child's genitals while in a movie. A child may be kidnapped and raped. Both boys and girls are commonly the victims of brief incidents of sexual abuse.

Continuing relationships

This type of sexual abuse occurs as a part of an ongoing relationship. The abuse starts gradually and continues for weeks, months or years. The abuser may be a neighbor who invites the child to his house to play regularly. It might be a teacher, pastor, camp counselor, family friend, or someone the child has met on the Internet. The victim may be a boy or a girl.

14

Incest

In this type of sexual abuse, the abuser is a member of the child's immediate family, usually a stepfather or older brother but sometimes a female. The victim is most often a girl. The abuse usually begins gradually but happens more often as time goes on. The abuse may go on for years until someone outside the family discovers it or until the child grows up and moves out of the house.

How do people use the Internet to sexually abuse children?

Some abusers find their victims on the Internet. They use chat rooms or websites to meet children and gain their trust. Then they may exchange sexual messages or pictures with their victims, or arrange face-to-face meetings to abuse them.

Abusers who exploit children through prostitution or pornography sometimes use the Internet to find other abusers who will use their services. They also use the Internet to find children to abuse through prostitution or pornography.

Some abusers use the Internet to meet other abusers. They share their views about child sexual abuse, ideas about how to find and abuse children, information about specific victims, or suggestions about how to avoid being caught or punished for their crimes.

How many children are victims of sexual abuse?

Statistics suggest that as many as one child in every three or four in the United States becomes the victim of sexual abuse by the time he or she reaches the age of 18. At least 25% of adults were victims of child sexual abuse. This means that millions of adults in the United States today were sexually abused as children.

At what age are children sexually abused?

Children may be abused at any age from infancy to adolescence. The most common age for sexual abuse to begin is age nine. Most sexual abuse is reported by teenagers, but they have usually been victimized for many years before finally reporting the abuse. Most sexual abuse, particularly that involving a continuing relationship or incest, starts before the child reaches puberty.

Are boys ever sexually abused?

Both boys and girls are the victims of sexual abuse. Girls are probably victimized more frequently. Approximately ten percent of all victims reporting sexual abuse are boys, but probably many, many more are abused.

Why doesn't the child victim report being sexually abused?

There are many reasons why children don't report that someone has sexually abused them. The very young child may not realize that the abuser is doing anything wrong. Children are taught to obey adults. The child may not realize at first that he or she should object.

Later the child may not tell anyone because of fear. He or she may fear the abuser or fear not being believed. The child may fear that he or she will be punished or blamed for the abuse or that some harm will come to the abuser. The victim of incest may fear that the family will be broken up if anyone finds out about the abuse. He or she may work very hard to keep it a secret.

Another reason that children don't tell anyone they have been sexually abused is because of their own feelings of shame and guilt. Child victims often believe that somehow the abuse is *their* fault.

Sometimes when children try to report sexual abuse, they are not believed. They then give up trying to tell anyone else. This is especially true if it is a parent who does not believe the child.

Do people ever forget being sexually abused as children, and then later remember these experiences?

One way the human mind protects itself from overwhelming emotional pain is by "forgetting" (repressing) bad memories. People who have been through extremely frightening or painful experiences, like wartime combat, natural disasters, torture, or sexual abuse, sometimes "forget" these experiences.

Later these painful memories may come back. This most often happens when the person feels strong enough to deal with the emotional pain of the traumatic event.

Can people ever have "false memories" of child sexual abuse?

People often remember the details of their experiences incorrectly. Sometimes people "remember" events that they imagined, or that someone convinced them really happened when it didn't. Although some people disagree, nearly all mental health professionals believe that most memories of child sexual abuse are true and generally accurate, however.

Why do people sexually abuse children?

Sexual abusers usually don't want to hurt the children they abuse. In fact, they often like children and try to please them. Many times abusers don't realize how much harm their behavior causes.

Many abusers are very self-centered people who have trouble considering anybody's welfare but their own. Because they enjoy the sexual activity, they believe the children do as well. Some abusers, because of their own selfishness, just don't care whether they harm the child or not. Some of these people may not abuse children directly, but arrange for others to abuse children sexually through prostitution or pornography, usually to make money.

Most direct sexual abusers have trouble relating to people their own age. Because they are often afraid or insecure in relationships with people their own age, they turn to children for companionship, friendship and sexual gratification. They feel safer and more comfortable in relationships with children because children are more trusting and easier to please or dominate than other adults.

Most people who sexually abuse children are not "crazy" but they do have serious psychological problems for which they need help. Many sexual abusers were victims of sexual abuse themselves as children.

Is the child victim to blame for the sexual abuse?

No! Even though many child victims feel guilty about being sexually abused, what happened was *not* their fault. The abuser is *totally* responsible for his or her own behavior.

Can a person who was sexually abused ever lead a "normal" life?

Yes! Most victims of child sexual abuse go on to lead very normal lives. They usually function well in most areas of everyday life. Victims of child sexual abuse have gotten themselves through some very tough situations. This is a real accomplishment! It suggests that such victims have some important strengths. Most victims of child sexual abuse make successful lives for themselves in spite of the hardships they have suffered.

However, the effects of child sexual abuse usually make their lives more difficult in some areas. Many times former victims do not realize that some of the problems they are having in their present lives are really the result of having been sexually abused as children. Once they realize this, working out the problems becomes easier. Even those having more serious problems can usually be helped by a professional counselor, and they can greatly improve their own lives.

Chapter Two
Understanding people who sexually abuse children

The victim often asks "Why me? Why did he *do* that to me?" Parents ask "How could she do that to my child! Why would anyone sexually abuse a child?"

Answering these questions is not easy. It is often difficult to understand why someone would sexually abuse a child. There are many different possible reasons but most of these reasons come down to the fact that the abuser has serious psychological problems. The abuser is more interested in satisfying his or her own needs than in protecting the welfare of the child. The abuser *uses* the child to make him or herself feel better in some way. The abuse is not a result of anything the child has done.

Many types of people sexually abuse children. Although we often think of a sexual abuser as a "dangerous stranger," this is usually not the case. About 80% of child victims are abused by someone they know rather than by a stranger.

Most sexual abusers are men or boys, although some are women or girls. Sexual abusers may be of any age from childhood to old age. Sexual abusers have many psychological problems. They are often individuals who do not feel comfortable with people their own age. They choose children to meet their needs because children are less threatening to them.

Most of what we know about sexual abusers comes from studies of men and boys who abuse children. Therefore, most of this discussion applies to male abusers because we have studied and understood them more completely.

Less is known about women and girls who sexually abuse children because sexual abuse by women is not reported often. Women abusers are usually involved in a continuing relationship or incest. Their victims are usually boys, although they sometimes abuse girls.

Women who sexually abuse children are usually "caretakers" for them, most often mothers or stepmothers. Sometimes they are nurses or teachers. They are usually very possessive and overprotective of their victims, yet very immature themselves. They depend on their victims to meet their own emotional needs.

Women who sexually abuse children usually are single. If they are married, their husbands are often gone from the home or emotionally distant. They probably abuse children to satisfy emotional rather than sexual needs.

Men who sexually abuse children in non-aggressive, non-violent ways are different from those who abuse children in violent, aggressive ways. In this chapter, these non-violent abusers will be called "child molesters" to distinguish them from the more violent abusers who will be called "rapists." Most sexual abuse of children is by child molesters rather than by rapists. Both child molesters and rapists have serious psychological problems.

Child molesters abuse children to meet their emotional and sexual needs. They are attracted to children as sex objects and are also seeking acceptance or companionship. Rapists use and abuse children through sexual acts mainly to satisfy other needs and desires. These needs include power, anger and sadistic feelings.

Relationships with other adults, especially sexual relationships, are usually very threatening to both rapists and child molesters. Their reactions to this threat are different, however. The child molester avoids the threat by turning to children as a safer substitute. The rapist denies his fears by striking out and attacking children.

Fixated child molesters

First, let us examine what we know about child molesters. One group of child molesters is called "fixated child molesters." This means that they are stuck or "fixated" at a child-like or adolescent level of psychological development.

Fixated child molesters have never developed the ability to relate comfortably to adults their own age, especially in sexual ways. They feel more comfortable with children and see themselves as "one of the kids" in many ways. Sometimes they assume parent-like roles as "protectors" or "teachers" of their victims.

The primary sexual orientation of fixated child molesters is toward children. They find children more sexually exciting than adults. Young boys are usually the victims of this type of abuser. Even though the victim is the same sex as the abuser, the child molester is usually not a homosexual. He does not find adult men (or adult women) sexually exciting. He is attracted to boys because they are children, not because they are males.

Fixated child molesters have little close involvement with other people their own age. Their sexual interest in children often begins in their adolescence. It is a persistent interest and their sexual activity with children often becomes compulsive. Even though they may want to stop or try to stop, they continue to sexually abuse children. Sexual contacts are usually planned carefully in advance. Alcohol or drug use is not usually related to the sexual abuse.

Fixated child molesters are people who have never grown up psychologically and socially. They may abuse children because children are the only people they feel comfortable with. Or, if the abuser was the victim of child sexual abuse himself, he may sexually abuse children because it allows him to feel like a powerful person instead of a victim.

Regressed child molesters

The other group of child molesters is called "regressed child molesters." These people have developed some social skills that allow them to interact with other adults, especially women. They often marry and have families of their own. When these people are under a great deal of stress however, they "regress" or move back to relationships with children.

The primary sexual orientation of regressed child molesters is toward people of their own age. They usually find adults more sexually exciting than children. However, they often have poor resources for handling stress. When crises or traumas occur in adulthood, they may become overwhelmed. They then turn to children to meet their emotional needs through sexual activity. They replace their difficult relationships with other adults with involvement with children.

The regressed child molester's sexual abuse of children may occur in cycles. He abuses children primarily when he is experiencing high levels of stress. During periods of low stress, the abuse may stop. He may also have sexual contacts with people his own age during the same period of time he is abusing the child. His sexual abuse of children is more likely to be impulsive at first, rather than planned out. Often it takes place when he has been drinking or using drugs. Alcohol is not the cause of the abuse, but its use "allows" the abuser to do things he might not otherwise do.

Regressed child molesters usually choose girls as their victims. The regressed child molester often imagines that the girl is much older than she really is. In his mind he thinks of her as an adult, and therefore she becomes an appropriate sexual partner.

Regressed child molesters are often involved in incest. As incest continues, the sexual abuser often abandons his role as parent while the victim gradually takes on responsibilities for keeping the family together and meeting the abuser's needs.

Rapists

Most sexual abuse of children is nonviolent, however sometimes children are forcibly raped. Rape is not primarily the result of sexual desire. It is a form of aggression expressed through sexual acts.

The motives for rapes are often divided into three categories: anger, power and sadism. Although each rape is usually dominated by one of these motives, some elements of the other two may also be present.

Rapists also act in special situations, which are somewhat different from other types of rape. One of these is gang rape when several people rape one person. A second situation is rape that occurs in institutions, particularly correctional institutions. A third is rape or other sexual abuse that occurs within a cult as a part of the rituals of the cult.

The anger rapist

The anger rapist attacks children (or adults) as a means of expressing or venting feelings of anger and rage. The rape is often physically brutal. The rapist is taking out his anger at other people, or at frustrating situations, on his victim. His intent is to hurt and debase his victim. Sometimes he makes the victim perform sexual acts that he considers degrading. Anger rapes tend to happen quickly. The rapist often acts without planning and then escapes.

The power rapist

The power rapist feels inadequate and insecure. His goal in rape is the sexual conquest and control of the victim. This makes him feel powerful. He uses only enough force as is necessary to get what he wants. The power rapist often sees himself as "winning" his victim rather than forcing himself on her. He needs to believe that the victim wanted to have sex with him and even enjoyed it. This way he can feel like an important, desirable, powerful person.

The sadistic rapist

Sadistic rapists are very rare but have severe psychological problems. For them, sexuality and aggression become mixed. They get sexual enjoyment and satisfaction from tormenting and injuring victims. Such rapes often end in murder.

The gang rapist

In gang rapes, each rapist may have a different motive. One may be venting his anger on the victim. Another may be trying to prove his power to the other rapists or to the victim. Still another may be trying to gain acceptance from his buddies.

The inmate rapist

In correctional institutions, rape is often one way
an inmate demonstrates his power over another
inmate. Although this usually involves sexual acts
between two people of the same sex, it has nothing
to do with homosexuality. An inmate rapes another
inmate to prove that he is powerful and dominant
over him, not because he finds him sexually
exciting.

Ritual rape within a cult

Rape or other sexual abuse of children sometimes
occurs as an acceptable, and even required, part of
the rituals within a cult. A cult leader may require
his followers to participate in ritual rape as a way of
reinforcing or proving his dominance over them.
Ritual rapists within a cult may be trying to
demonstrate their loyalty to the cult or to the cult
leader. Ritual rapists may also be trying to
"educate" children growing up within the cult to
increase their loyalty and dependence on the cult
through fear and domination.

Sociopaths

Other motives for the sexual abuse of children do
exist, especially among "sociopaths," who are
individuals with an "Antisocial Personality
Disorder." This type of person is extremely self-
centered and cares little for the welfare of others.
His own desires are more important.

The sociopath may be a very charming, clever and interesting person. Often he becomes involved in other criminal activities. Having sex with children may be just one of the many types of sexual activities he tries.

A sociopath may sexually abuse children "for kicks." He is always looking for excitement. He may not be especially interested in children as sexual objects but, rather, may be interested in the excitement of a new experience.

Other sociopaths may sexually abuse children because children are easily available to satisfy a sexual need. These sociopaths usually become involved in brief incidents of sexual abuse, although involvement in a continuing relationship or incest is also possible.

Still other sociopaths may sexually abuse children indirectly for profit. They do not have sex with the children themselves, but involve the children in prostitution or in making pornography. These sociopaths care more about the money they can make exploiting children than about the harm they cause their child victims.

Common characteristics

Whatever motivations lead an individual to sexually abuse children, these individuals often have characteristics in common.

- Many of them were victims of sexual or physical abuse themselves as children.

29

- Most of them are self-centered and think more about satisfying their own needs than about the welfare of the children they abuse.

- Most of them "feel bad" if they realize they are harming their victims, but this is not enough to cause them to stop the sexual abuse.

- Most sexual abusers of children will continue to do this until they are stopped by outside intervention.

- People who sexually abuse children have serious psychological problems. They can often be helped through professional treatment, however. This treatment usually takes a long time and requires much effort on the part of the abuser. Without treatment, the abuser is most likely to continue abusing children even though he or she may not wish to do so.

Many sexual abusers are sent to prison if their crimes are discovered. Some are sent to hospitals for treatment. It is possible for some abusers to receive treatment on an outpatient basis. The success of treatment always depends on how highly motivated the abuser is to change his or her behavior.

Did your experience include any people like these?

Think about the person who sexually abused you. Do any of these descriptions seem to fit him or her? Understanding the reasons people sexually abuse children can help you realize that the abuse you suffered was due to the psychological problems of the abuser.

The abuse was not your fault.

Chapter Three
Stories from victims of child sexual abuse

When something bad happens to you, it often helps to know that you are not the only one. You feel better if you know that other people have had the same kinds of problems. Here are some experiences other victims of child sexual abuse have had. Some were victims of brief incidents of sexual abuse. Others were victims of sexual abuse as part of a continuing relationship. Still others were victims of incest. All of these stories are true. The names and some of the details have been changed to protect the privacy of the victims.

Brief incidents

Brief incidents of child sexual abuse can take many forms. Some have great impact on the victim and others have little effect. Many children, both boys and girls, are victimized in these ways. Here are some of their stories.

Connie, age 33

I have always been terrified of hospitals, but I never knew why. Then one day it came back to me. When I was 12, I had my tonsils out. I remember a nurse came into my room one night after my parents had gone home. I was half asleep because of medication. She started rubbing my head, then my body under the sheet. She massaged my breasts, then my thighs and pubic area. I was scared and felt so helpless. I just "froze" until she quit and went away. I have had this really emotional reaction to hospitals ever since but had blocked out that whole incident.

Carlos, age 16

I was at the beach one day when I was about 12. I was all alone in the changing room when this old man came in. He came over to me while I was starting to put on my swimming trunks. He grabbed for me but I got away and ran home. I don't go back there alone anymore.

Tina, age 13

I was walking along the road and this guy stopped in a van. He offered me a ride and I said, "No, I am almost home." Then he opened the door and grabbed me by the arm and pulled me in. I was too scared to run. He told me to shut up and sit there. We drove out into the hills and he raped me. He did it twice. He kept saying he knew I liked it. Then he drove me back to town and let me out in the park. I walked home crying.

My mom kept asking me what was wrong until I told her. She told my dad and he went wild. I was afraid he was going to hit me, but he kept saying he was just mad at the guy.

They took me to the hospital for an examination. I don't remember much. Then we went to the police station. They were really nice, but they just kept asking me the same questions over and over like they didn't believe me.

The worst part was going back to school. Everybody asked me dumb questions and I felt like a freak. They all knew what had happened. They looked at me weird. I just felt dirty. I'd be sitting there in class and like a dream it would be happening again. I'd see the man and the van. I'd just sit there shaking.

I got real upset when we had to go to the preliminary hearing. I couldn't sleep and then I threw up just before court. I'm so scared that they will let the guy out.

Glenda, age 16

It was really weird. I had just gotten my driver's license and we went over to this older guy's house. There were three of us girls. They knew him, but I didn't. He gave us some beer and some pot. We were having a good time. Then he started joking around and trying to undress us. He said I could take his Mustang out for a drive once he "got to know me." We were being silly and were mainly in our underwear then. He was being real friendly, acting silly and tickling us.

He showed us his bedroom and he had a video camera by the bed. He wanted us to get on the bed and do things with each other while he filmed it. I wouldn't do it though and I felt real weird and left.

35

They stayed, but the next day they said they hadn't done anything. I felt so dirty after that. Wow! If anybody knew what I had been doing there I would have died. He said lots of girls had done that stuff for him, but I don't know. I've been so afraid the other girls would tell somebody what we were doing.

Greg, age 20

I was twelve years old when they put me in the juvenile detention center the first time. I had just been hanging around and the cops picked me up for curfew violation. I spent the night there and most of the next day.

That night, after the guard had left, the other guy in my room started hassling me. He was bigger but not a lot older, just tough. He wanted me to masturbate him but I wouldn't. Finally he backed me up against the wall and said, "You've got three seconds, sucker! Go down or die!" I did what he wanted, then he left me alone. I lay awake all night though, scared to death of him.

Marti, age 19

It was just about when I started kindergarten. There was a bigger boy in the neighborhood that always kind of hung around. One afternoon he came in the yard and asked if I wanted to see his puppy. He said it was in a shed down the alley. I went to see, but there was no puppy. He gave me

36

some chewing gum and said he was going to play a game. He took my clothes off and set me up on a box. He mainly just looked at me and licked and kissed me. Then he gave me a whistle and told me not to tell anybody and left.

My mom found me there. Then it seemed like it was all my fault or something. They got real upset and made me go with them to tell his mother. They called the cops and did a lot of yelling. I really didn't have much of an idea what was going on, but I knew it was bad.

They wouldn't let me even play outside after that. Then they wouldn't say anything about it anymore. I couldn't even mention it. I always had the feeling something awful must have happened to me, or I had done something awful, but I just couldn't figure it out.

Shawn, age 32

One time we had a babysitter. I guess he was a neighbor kid. I was only about seven or eight. He came into the bathroom when I was in there. He took out his penis and started rubbing it. He tried to get me to touch it, but I told him to go away. I never said anything to my mother about it 'cause I didn't know what to say. We never had him as a babysitter anymore though.

Rod, age 42

I was sexually abused when I was a kid. It happened several times, always by men. One time was in a restroom at the bus station. Another time coming home from school, a gang of young boys grabbed me and pulled all my clothes off. Somebody came by and stopped them before they did anything else though.

It has always made me wonder if there was something wrong with me. For a long time it made me wonder if I was a homosexual or something.

Continuing Relationships

Sexual abuse often takes place in the context of a continuing relationship. It may go on for a long time before anyone finds out. The child victim often knows, likes and trusts the abuser. Parents are usually very surprised when they find out what has been happening. Parents usually think of a child molester as a dangerous stranger, not as someone who might be a relative, neighbor or family friend. Some of the stories of these victims are examples of trusting relationships being used for sexual abuse.

Carmen, age 15

I don't know why it always happens to me. There must have been something wrong with me, I mean. There must be something special about me that I am chosen. It must be my fault. It seems like it has happened a lot to me.

The first time was when I was ten. My cousin and I were playing out in the woods. He is three years older than I am. We started playing around and kidding. We just touched each other and stuff like that. It was fun at first. Every time after that, we'd play together, we'd go out in the woods and do that. At least he would want to. I started to think that I really shouldn't do it. I started to feel bad, like something was wrong.

For two or three years we would keep doing it though because I didn't know how to say no. I just tried to stay away from him or stay around the other people when he was there. He told me he would tell if I didn't go with him though. Finally they moved away. Now I only see him in the summers sometimes and nothing happens.

It happened again, or at least it almost happened, one time when my father brought his boss home. We went out in the back yard and he started putting his arm around me and telling me how pretty I was. I didn't like it, but I just sort of froze. Then he felt my breasts and tried to kiss me and I ran away. I stayed in my room the whole night and told my parents I was sick.

Another time there was a flasher by the school. I was with a couple of other girls and he flashed me. We ran away, ran home, but didn't tell anybody.

Now I'm afraid it's going to happen again. It's just something about me that makes it happen. My mother has a friend who comes over a lot. They're going to real estate school together. He always talks to me and he's real nice. Sometimes he rubs my back, which is nice, but I can tell he wants to do more. Sometimes I'd like him to, but I usually just feel dirty when he touches me. I feel like I want to throw up. I'm not going to let him do anything like that to me, but I still don't know what to do. You would think my mother would stop him, but she doesn't even seem to notice. She's too busy with her studying.

John, age 25

I was 12 when my mother started going with Chip. He was real nice to me for a while. He used to take me out to the racetrack to watch the stock cars. He would buy me lots of stuff, candy and sodas and stuff.

Then one day when my mom wasn't at home, he threw me down on the bed and raped me. He told me he was going to have me and started taking down his pants. At first I tried to fight, but he was much stronger and did just what he wanted. It really hurt, but he didn't care. He told me if I ever told anybody he'd kill me.

I was so scared, I didn't say anything. Not for a long time. He was over at the house most of the time. He never really lived there though. But any time my mom left, he'd come after me. I would just lie there and take it. I'd think about all the things I would do to him. I hated him. I wanted to kill him.

One time I even got a gun. I put it in the drawer by the bed. That was when I was older. I had it there right near the bed. I thought I would shoot him.

That would make him stop, but I was chicken. I hated the way he looked. I hated the way he talked. I still want to kill him. If I found him now, I would.

That went on for about two years. He finally got in some kind of trouble and left town. We never heard from him anymore and I think he's lucky. Nothing like that ever happened to me again, but it's in my mind all the time. The hate is always there.

Teresa, age 34

My childhood was really rough. That was mainly because my uncle and brother sexually molested me. When I was ten or eleven, my uncle started doing it. He would come into the house when nobody was there. Usually he'd be drunk. He would chase me around and grab me. I'd try to run away but there was nothing I could do. This went on for about a year. It probably happened seven or eight times. I told my mom about it, but she didn't believe me. It was her brother.

Then later my brother tried the same thing. I don't remember when. I blocked it out. Later my brother-in-law tried to rape me once, but I threw him out. I've always had problems with men, problems with relationships. My relationships with men always go bad.

Until the sixth grade I made good grades, A's and B's. Then I started getting bad grades and getting in trouble a lot at school. I had social problems with my friends and with men. I felt like I was alone and nobody wanted me. I started doing things, goofing off, things that got me in trouble.

Mom took me to a counselor when I was in junior high school because of problems with friends and because I was constantly depressed. I cut my wrists when I was 13 or 14. I just wanted to give up. That seemed like the only way.

Candy, age 8

He was nice to me before, but he was a bad man. My daddy said he was. He lives right next door. I used to play at his house a lot. He gave me birthday presents. Sometimes he came over to barbeques at our house, but mostly I saw him at his house.

When we watched TV, he would hold me on his lap and hug me. Sometimes he put his hand in my pants and rubbed me so that it felt good. He didn't ever hurt me but he said we would keep it a secret. He was only nice like that to special little girls.

He had a secret drawer too. He showed it to me, and if I was really good, he would let me open it. There was always some kind of candy in it and we would eat it. We kept that a secret too 'cause I'm not supposed to eat candy between meals.

I used to see him lots of times, ever since I was little. He didn't do that other stuff until just a while ago. Sometimes I didn't like it and he would stop. Sometimes I didn't like the things he did. Sometimes it hurt. I got scared sometimes. He said if I told anybody, I couldn't come over anymore. They'd be mad at him. One time my mommy came to get me when I was on his lap. I was scared she would find out, but she didn't.

I told my friend Carol what he did. She used to come with me sometimes but he only hugged and tickled her. She didn't get any of the candy either. The drawer was a secret from her too. She told her mother and she told my mother. I can't go over there anymore.

They put him in jail, I think. He's mean and bad. I guess I was bad too. I hope they don't put me in jail. He's home now, but I don't talk to him. They said he hurt me, but it mostly didn't hurt. I guess he's mad at me. He doesn't wave at me even when I wave at him, so now I stick my tongue out at him.

Stacey, age 16

I used to play with my cousins a lot. They were boys about five years older than I was. When I was about ten, they were over at my house one day when no one else was there. My mother had gone to the grocery store. We were playing around and then they covered me up with a blanket and made me undress. They kept me covered but put their hands under the blanket and felt me. They felt my body in all sorts of ways. I didn't like it and told them to let me go, but they wouldn't stop.

I was too ashamed to tell my mother after that, but I didn't want to be alone with them anymore. Sometimes it would happen though, even though I tried to stay away from them. They did stuff like that two or three more times. Then I just wouldn't stay with them anymore. I never told anybody about it. I felt weird and dirty after that.

Now my boyfriend is friends with one of my cousins. He doesn't know what happened to me though. Sometimes he wants us all to go out to play pool together or for a pizza. If I say no, I can't tell him why, and he gets mad. So we go out sometimes with my cousin, but I always feel sick and dirty around him.

Sometimes I feel dirty and sick when my boyfriend touches me. Then I get mad at myself. I wish I had done something about what they had done to me, but I don't know what.

Incest

Many children are sexually abused through incest. Some statistics suggest that as many as one child in every 100 is the victim of incest. Most don't tell anyone about the abuse until they get older. Some never tell.

Jackie's story is typical of many girls who are sexually abused by their fathers or stepfathers. She was abused by her stepfather for many years before she told anyone. The abuse started gradually but became more frequent and open as time went on. Her mother did little to stop the abuse. Jackie finally reported it as a teenager. Then she was removed from the home. Her stepfather was convicted of child sexual abuse and placed on probation on the condition that he obtain psychological treatment.

Jackie, age 18

My stepfather was the one who did it. He started
when I was about six, I guess. He would come in to
tuck me in at night and sometimes just run his
hand over my body. It felt good and I didn't think
that was anything wrong.

Later on Daddy started doing other things with his
hands. That didn't seem right but I was supposed to
obey him. Then he started kissing me and kissing
me under the covers. I must have been ten by then.

I was frightened. I knew my mother would punish
me if she found out and I knew Daddy would be
mad at me, too. I felt like it was my fault, but I
didn't understand how. I didn't want anyone to find
out how bad I was.

I remember lying awake in the dark hoping he
wouldn't come. I told myself I would jump up and
run if he came, but I never did. I just lay there and
hoped he would go away soon. Then I would cry
and finally go to sleep. But then I would have
nightmares about monsters.

One night my mother came in and saw him. She got
real mad. He cried and promised never to do it
again. She never said anything to me, but I always
felt like she was mad at me too. We started to go to
church then. He went every night they had a
service.

Nothing happened again until I was 12. The he started being real nice to me again. By then I was doing a lot of the work around the house. My mother was always tired. She just never seemed very happy. My stepfather and I always had a good time together though. We would go to the grocery store to pick up whatever we needed for dinner. It would be just me and him. My brothers and sisters would stay at home. Sometimes he'd buy me something special on those trips. He always took my part with my younger brother and sisters. They knew they couldn't mess with me when he was around. It was pretty nice sometimes, the special way he treated me.

Then he started coming into my room again at night. I don't think my mother ever knew about it. He would cry sometimes and say he loved me. He said they'd split up the family if anybody knew what was happening. He said my mom would probably get real sick if she ever found out.

He didn't come in very often. Just a couple of times a month maybe. I started lying awake again waiting for him, hating it. I was so ashamed. What if other people found out? My brothers and sisters said I was the favorite. What if they knew what I had done?

I felt so rotten, like I was all alone and always would be. How could I ever tell anybody about anything so awful? I thought about running away or killing myself, but I was afraid to do either one. I wished someone would stop him, but I knew I had to keep doing what he wanted or terrible things would happen.

My mom even asked me once if he ever did "those things" to me again. I couldn't let her know, so I said no. If she had cared more, it seems like she would have checked more though. I guess she just didn't care as long as I didn't cause her any problems.

Then the trouble started when I wanted to go out with boys. He started getting real mean about letting me leave the house alone. He would make me turn down dates and, when I turned 15, he wouldn't let me get a driver's license. He said it gave me too much freedom. He was always asking who I was with, what I was doing and would get mad if boys called me on the phone. Sometimes I saw him in the car following us when I did go out.

He would do all sorts of nice things for me though. He gave me money any time I wanted it and would buy me clothes if I wanted. I would get sick about myself though. It was like I was selling myself to him for the things I wanted to do. I couldn't tell anybody then because I hadn't said anything before. They would just say I was a whore. Maybe I was. I felt so rotten. My mother was mad at me a lot because she said he would do anything I asked. I knew she'd be mad if she found out why.

Then he put me on restriction just because I came home late from the movies. I wasn't even with a boy, but he still got mad. He said I couldn't go anywhere for a month and then he slapped me and called me a tramp. I was real scared and mad at him and mad at my mom.

The next day in school I kept crying and they took me to the counselor. First I told her it was because my stepdad had slapped me, but then I told her the truth. Then everything got to be a big mess. She called the cops and they arrested him. He didn't stay in jail long though.

Everybody is mad at me now. I'm living with my aunt and I'm not supposed to see him anymore. I know what he did was wrong, but sometimes I still feel like I am to blame. It is hard to shake the feeling that I caused all these problems. I wonder if I will ever feel different.

Jackie's experience

Jackie's feelings and behaviors are very common for victims of incest. The reactions of children to incest are so common that they even have a special name, "Child Sexual Abuse Accommodation Syndrome." These reactions are all the *normal* responses of *normal* children who are sexually abused. They are different from what other people expect, however. The difference between how children react normally and how people expect a sexually abused child to react makes it harder for the child to be believed if he or she finally does report the sexual abuse.

At first the child victim keeps the sexual abuse secret because of her confusion, fears and feelings of guilt and shame. She feels helpless. She feels powerless to stop the sexual advances of an adult she depends on. So, she does nothing, often pretending to be asleep in her bed at night while he abuses her.

As the abuse continues she adjusts to it and is trapped by it. She comes to believe she is the guilty person who deserves to be punished by the abuse. It becomes her duty to keep the family together by submitting to the abuse and keeping it a secret.

Finally, often after many years of abuse, she may report it. This often comes after a fight with the abuser. Often the authorities do not believe her claims of being abused because her secrecy, helplessness, immobility and the adjustments she has made do not seem like normal reactions to other people. Therefore they often do not believe that sexual abuse could have taken place the way she claims.

If she is believed, she is often the one removed from the home. Many times criminal charges are not brought against the abuser because there is not enough proof. As a final step, the victim is often pressured by family members to take back her claims of abuse. She gives in to the pressure, changes her story, and this lie is quickly believed.

This Child Sexual Abuse Accommodation Syndrome is seen in many, many cases of father-daughter incest. Some of its elements can be seen in other types of incest or other patterns of sexual abuse, as well.

Mary Ellen's experience

Sometimes incest occurs between a child and her older brother. Mary Ellen and her younger sister were sexually abused by an older brother. Although she complained to her father, he would believe nothing bad about his son. The sexual abuse continued several years before Mary Ellen finally worked up the courage to report the abuse to authorities. Her father was extremely angry and blamed her for "getting the family in trouble." It took a long time for Mary Ellen to believe she had done the right thing in reporting the situation and saving herself and her sister from further abuse. Her father's blame hurt as much as the effects of the abuse.

Mary Ellen, age 16

My brother sexually abused us, me and my younger sister. I think he might have done it to one of my older sisters too, but I don't know. He started when I was ten. That's when my older sister left home.

He made me fellate him. That's what the lawyer says you call it. He did that lots. It made me sick to have that in my mouth, but if I didn't do it he hit me. He used to do things to my sister when she was in bed. She didn't say anything, but I saw him sometimes.

I told my dad but he wouldn't believe me. He never thought Rick did anything wrong. Maybe he just didn't care. He was drunk a lot. He said we would grow up to be tramps anyway. We couldn't go out of the house hardly. He said we would just chase boys and get pregnant. My stepmom didn't care either. I think maybe she and Rick used to do stuff, have sex together sometimes.

I got so I was scared to come home after school. I thought about telling somebody for a long time. I told him I would tell, but he said I'd be sorry, that he would just say that I was a tramp and then everyone would know what a slut I was. I think that's what people think now. They talk a lot at school about why I moved out. By the time I finally told anybody, that's what I felt like—like I was a slut for letting it go on so long. I had to do something. My dad probably won't ever see it my way though. I hope he'll change his mind. He just starts yelling when we visit though.

Jessica's experience

Sometimes incest is reported early in its course, before it has time to continue for long. The effects can still be traumatic for the victim. Both the effects of the abuse and the family disruption that occurs when it is reported can cause the victim to suffer. Jessica was only four years old when she was removed from her family following sexual abuse by an older brother. The family refused to believe that he had abused Jessica. She was living with a foster family when she told this story. It is too early yet to know how these experiences will affect her as she gets older.

Jessica, age 4

My brother Danny did it. He did it in the shed. He tried to put his thing in me. He hurt me. He hurt me where I go to the bathroom. He said he'd give me the Smurf hat if I went in the shed, but he never did. He lied to me. He did bad things. He did them that day and he did them another day. He told me not to tell. I didn't tell anybody. I just told my friend. Her mother told then. They took me to live with somebody else. I like it there. They have lots of swings, but I miss my mommy. Do you think my mommy still loves me? I don't think so. She said Danny didn't do that, but he did. My mommy doesn't like me anymore. I miss my mommy.

William's experience

Although it is not as common, sometimes boys are the victims of incest. William's teenage stepmother began abusing him when he was six. The abuse ended only when he was sent to a military school at age ten because of "unmanageable" behavior. As an adult, he has finally been able to sort out the many confusing feelings he experienced during those years and the ones that followed.

William, age 23

She was quite a lady, my stepmother. She was only sixteen, just a child herself. My father was wild, off working on oilrigs or getting thrown in jail. When he was gone, she wouldn't take care of us, me and my brother. We'd have to go to the neighbor's and ask for something to eat. When he was home she was sweet as pie to us. We tried to tell Dad, but he whipped us for making up lies.

Then she started being real sweet to me. I was only six. What does a kid that age know? She'd take me to bed with her and hug and kiss me. She taught me to do all sorts of things to her—all sexual. Every day, every way, I had to do it all for her. I thought it meant she loved me. At least she wasn't knocking me down the stairs like she did my brother.

I never told my dad about those things. Somehow I knew I had to keep them secret, or I'd lose her. Even when they sent me away I thought she still loved me. She kissed me goodbye and smiled. I knew anything that was wrong was my fault. She really screwed up my ideas about love and about myself.

Was your experience like any of these?

All these people were victims of sexual abuse when they were children. Was what happened to you like any of the things that happened to them? Did you feel any of the same emotions? Did you think or do any of the same things they did?

The next chapter discusses some of the emotions that victims of child sexual abuse often feel and some of the problems sexual abuse may cause.

Chapter Four
The effects of child sexual abuse on the victim and the victim's family

Child sexual abuse affects the way a victim thinks, feels and acts. Confusion is often the victim's first reaction. Many times the victim also feels strong and frightening emotions. The victim may come to believe bad things about him or herself and about other people because of the sexual abuse. As a result, the behavior of the victim may change in many ways.

This chapter discusses many of the ways a victim thinks, feels and acts as a result of child sexual abuse. It also discusses the reactions of the victim's family.

Confusion

Surprise and confusion are often the first reactions of a victim of child sexual abuse. He or she thinks, "What is going on? Is this right or wrong? What should I do? Will it happen again? Should I tell someone? Why do I feel so funny? Why is this happening to me?"

It is natural to be confused when something happens that you don't understand. Children cannot be expected to know how to respond to sexual abuse, unless they have been taught what to

55

do. The child's confusion is one weapon the abuser uses against the child to take advantage of him or her.

Even after the child victim grows up, some confusion about the sexual abuse may remain. That is one reason why it is helpful for a victim to learn as much as possible about child sexual abuse. In this way the victim often finds answers to many of the questions he or she has had for so long.

In addition to being confused about the sexual abuse, the victim may also be confused about the many different emotions he or she has been feeling. It is confusing to feel so many emotions at the same time. Sorting them out and understanding each one is hard. This chapter will help you make sense of some of the emotions you may have felt.

Many times victims of child sexual abuse worry about the emotions they feel. Sometimes they are frightened by them or ashamed of them. It is normal for victims to have many, many emotions: some pleasant, some unpleasant, and some even frightening to think about or to feel. All of these emotions are normal reactions to being a victim of child sexual abuse.

Just what kinds of feelings or emotions do children have when they are victims of sexual abuse? Children often feel anger, fear, shame and guilt. Let's talk about each one of these feelings.

Anger

The child victim often feels anger. The victim may
be angry at the abuser because of what he or she is
doing. The victim may be angry at him or herself for
not knowing what to do about the abuse. The victim
may be angry at his or her parents for not
preventing the abuse or for not taking action to stop
it from happening again. The victim may be angry
at anybody and everybody because of what has
happened.

Often, when a girl is being abused by her father or
stepfather, she tries to tell her mother what is
happening. Many times her mother is afraid to
become involved because *she* doesn't know what to
do. Sometimes the mother will say she doesn't
believe her daughter, or that what is happening is
the daughter's fault. Then the mother will not do
anything to stop the sexual abuse.

Other times the mother tries to stop it, but she
cannot without telling other people. Then she may
do nothing because she is ashamed of what her
husband is doing or she may be afraid of breaking
up the family. So the abuse continues. The victim in
this kind of situation often feels much anger toward
her mother.

Some victims are frightened by their own anger.
They are afraid that if they start to express their
anger, it will be so strong that they will do
something violent.

Fear

Many children who are the victims of sexual abuse feel fear. There are many things to fear. The child may be afraid of being hurt by the abuser, especially if the abuser threatens this. The child may fear that he or she has been physically damaged in some way by the sexual abuse. The child may be afraid of not being believed if he or she does tell someone about the abuse. The child may be afraid of some harm coming to the offender or to someone else in the family if the abuse is discovered.

The child may be afraid the family will break up or may be afraid of losing the friendship and love of the abuser or of another family member. The child may be afraid of being blamed for the abuse. The child may be afraid of being arrested or punished for having done something wrong. The child may be afraid of having to talk to strangers about the abuse or of testifying in court if charges are filed against the abuser. The child may be frightened of being abused again.

Sometimes there are so many fears that the child begins to feel fearful all the time without being able to identify exactly what it is that is feared. This constant unidentified fear makes life very difficult for the child. Sometimes these feelings of fear and anxiety stay with the victim for a long time.

Shame

Shame is another emotion the child victim often feels. He or she may feel "dirty." The victim may feel he or she is the only person such a thing has ever happened to and that he or she is different from everyone else. The victim fears that other people will find out how different, or how dirty, or how bad he or she really is. The victim believes no one would like or care about him or her if anyone knew about the sexual abuse.

Guilt

The child victim of sexual abuse frequently feels guilty for what is happening. The victim may believe that the sexual abuse is his or her fault. This is especially true if the abuse was ever pleasurable or if the abuser gave the child special rewards. The victim may believe that he or she did something to bring on the abuse or feel guilty because he or she did not try hard enough to stop the abuse. The victim may feel guilty for any good feelings toward the abuser or for bad feelings toward family members who were not helpful enough.

If the victim does report the abuse, many of the results can cause feelings of guilt in the victim. Sometimes the abuser is put in prison. Other times, when the abuser is a parent, the marriage may end in divorce and the family may be split up. The victim often feels guilty, believing that he or she has caused all of this to happen. This is especially true if other family members blame the victim.

All of these emotions are common reactions of children who have been sexually abused. Perhaps you can identify some of these emotions in the victims who told their stories in Chapter Two. Have you felt any of these emotions? Do you worry about having these emotions? Each person has a right to his or her own feelings. All of these emotions, and many others, are normal reactions to sexual abuse.

Other problems, in addition to strong and unpleasant emotions, can result from child sexual abuse. Some of the physical and psychological problems that child sexual abuse can cause are discussed next.

Physical problems

Sexual abuse can physically injure a child. The abuse may bruise or tear the genital areas. Infections can occur. The abuser may give a sexually transmitted disease (STD), such as gonorrhea, syphilis, HIV-AIDS or herpes to the child. Sometimes a child will be physically abused at the same time he or she is sexually abused. Some girls become pregnant because of sexual abuse. However, in spite of these possibilities, there is no physical injury to the child in most cases of child sexual abuse.

Psychological problems

Psychological distress of the victim is the most common effect of child sexual abuse. This distress can range from very mild to very severe. Many factors determine how severe the effects will be. Each person is different. Each situation is different.

Some general trends do appear, however.

- The psychological effects of child sexual abuse are usually greater when the abuse has involved physical violence.

- The psychological distress is usually greater if the child was abused by a trusted person rather than by a stranger.

- Brief incidents of child sexual abuse usually have less impact than abuse that continues over a long period of time.

- Children abused when they are very young usually show fewer psychological effects than children abused when they are older.

- The reactions of the family members and others around the victim greatly affect the psychological impact of the sexual abuse on the victim. Calm, supportive reactions from family members can reduce the effects of the abuse. Disorganized, disruptive and extreme responses from family members can create further psychological problems for the victim.

Three stages: Crisis, Suffering, Resolution

Any time something bad happens to someone, he or she goes through three stages of psychological experiences. The first is called the Crisis Stage. The second is called the Suffering Stage. The third is called the Resolution Stage.

These three stages, Crisis, Suffering, and Resolution, are not entirely separate from each other. Sometimes parts of two stages are present at the same time. Sometimes the victim moves back and forth between two stages.

The Crisis Stage

As soon as something bad happens, the Crisis Stage begins. Behavior becomes disorganized. Shock and denial set in. "I can't believe it!" "It didn't seem like it was really happening." "Why me?" "I panicked." "I couldn't think." These are common reactions to a bad event. Strong emotions are felt, or no emotions at all. The person may become unable to act, may act in a disorganized way, or may act in a cold, detached way. Shaking, nausea, crying or fainting may occur. This stage may last from a few minutes to a few days or longer.

The Suffering Stage

The second stage after a traumatic event is called the Suffering Stage because that is what happens: the victim suffers. Once the reality of the bad event sinks in, the victim starts to suffer emotionally.

Common reactions to sexual abuse during the Suffering Stage include excessive fears, nightmares, bedwetting, unrelated physical aches and pains, frequent memories of the abuse and "flashbacks" when it seems as if the events are happening all over again. Sometimes the victim "forgets" briefly that the bad event has happened. Victims often have trouble sleeping or trouble with their memory. They may have difficulty concentrating on things going on around them. Sometimes they lose interest in things they used to enjoy. Often they feel isolated from other people. They feel frightened and lose confidence in themselves. The victim may feel anger, fear, guilt, shame or depression.

This is a painful time for the victim. The victim goes over and over the events in his or her mind. Moods may change rapidly. One day things seem fine and the next day everything seems worse than ever.

The Suffering Stage usually lasts longer than the Crisis Stage. If the sexual abuse continues, the suffering continues. Even after the abuse ends, the suffering continues. Gradually, as time passes and the victim works through his or her thoughts and feelings about the event, the suffering decreases. Then the victim is entering the third stage.

The Resolution Stage

This third stage is the Resolution Stage. The victim does not forget what happened, but the event no longer seems to affect his or her life so greatly all the time. The event can be remembered without severe pain and distress. The victim has "learned to live with" what happened. It becomes one of the many experiences the person has had, some good and some bad. The former victim is now ready to go on with life.

If the resolution is a positive one, the victim comes out of the experience as a stronger individual who can view him or herself as a capable, worthwhile person. He or she has faced a difficult problem and has overcome it. This person can meet the challenges of everyday life and can enjoy family, friends, work or school and leisure activities. Recovery has taken place. The victim has become a successful survivor.

Sometimes the resolution is a negative one. Then the victim goes on living but continues to have difficulties in many areas of life. He or she remains a victim of the sexual abuse. Feelings of confusion, anger, fear, shame or guilt about the sexual abuse can stay with the victim for many years. Sometimes this leads to depression and thoughts of suicide. Other times it leads to the acting out of negative emotions in antisocial ways, that is, getting in trouble at home, at school or with the law.

These feelings can also create a very bad self-image in the victim. Being treated badly by the abuser may convince the child victim that he or she is ugly, bad, helpless and worthless. Such children come to believe that no one could ever love or care about them. Sometimes this leads victims to allow themselves to be used by other people in unhealthy ways. Occasionally, this leads to sexual promiscuity or prostitution. Women who are sexually abused as children often choose mates who are likely to abuse them physically and abuse their children as well.

After being the victim of sexual abuse, it is often difficult for the victim to trust other people. Difficulties in relationships may arise later in life, particularly with people of the same sex or physical appearance as the abuser. Sometimes when the victim becomes an adult, he or she has problems even in a desired sexual relationship. The child victim may have gotten the idea that anything having to do with sex is evil and shameful and has never changed this belief as an adult.

Some victims suffer from extreme nervousness or anxiety for many years as a result of the sexual abuse. Other victims have trouble later with their memory, particularly if they try to "block out" the bad memories. They may be unable to remember parts of their past lives at times. Occasionally, some victims retreat into their own private world and lose contact with reality.

Victims of incest often have poor ideas about the proper roles of parent and child. As children they assume too much responsibility in the family. As adults they have a poor idea of how a parent should behave, which makes it difficult for them to be good parents to their own children. Sometimes this leads to physical abuse.

Sometimes the only way a female incest victim knows how to relate to a male is sexually. The incest victim may have had little social contact with people her own age. She may not know how to act around other children. As a teenager or adult she may continue to feel "out of place" with others her own age because she has not developed good social skills. Victims often act older than their age but feel very insecure.

Victims of child sexual abuse occasionally become sexual abusers themselves. While most victims of sexual abuse never sexually abuse other children, some do. Most sexual abusers were themselves the victims of sexual abuse at one time.

All of these problems can result from a negative resolution. However, with help, these negative resolutions can be reversed and recovery achieved.

Difficulties preventing recovery

Sometimes, rather than achieving resolution and recovery, the victim gets stuck in the first or second stage. The victim may block the entire unpleasant event out of his or her mind for months or even years. This is one way the mind protects itself from pain, but it prevents the victim from progressing past the Crisis Stage toward recovery.

Sometimes the Suffering Stage goes on for many months or years. This happens when the victim is not able to work things out in a way that makes sense to him or her. It can also happen if the victim continues to blame him or herself for what happened. Then a professional counselor may be needed to help the victim get back on the road to recovery.

It helps to understand these three stages and to know that resolution and recovery are possible even if it doesn't seem so at first. When you are in the Crisis Stage, it is hard to believe you will ever feel better but you can accomplish this. It will take some effort on your part to make it happen, however.

Which stage are you in right now? Maybe you can see some elements from all three stages in yourself. Have you seen yourself progressing toward resolution in any way? Do you see some indications of a positive resolution in yourself? Are any indications of a negative resolution present?

Effects on the family

Child sexual abuse affects the victims' families as well as the victims themselves. Of course this is true when incest is involved. It is also true for other types of child sexual abuse as well.

Other family members often experience the same kinds of emotions as the victim. They may feel confusion, fear, anger, shame or guilt. Parents may blame themselves for not preventing the abuse and feel guilty for this. Family members are often very angry at the abuser. Occasionally, family members blame the victim for what happened.

Seeing other family members so upset can further disturb the child victim. The victim may hesitate to discuss the sexual abuse with family members because the victim fears upsetting them even more.

67

Family members may not know how to talk about the sexual abuse because they are embarrassed or frightened of the subject. Sometimes they discourage the victim from talking about the abuse, hoping it will be forgotten. Then the victim gets the idea that what happened was something too horrible to even talk about!

Sometimes other family members have been victims of sexual abuse themselves in the past and the new abuse brings back many unpleasant memories for them. If they have not achieved a positive resolution to the abuse they suffered, their own problems may increase because of the new abuse.

Luckily, some families reassure and support the victim. They try to understand how the victim feels and what has happened. They allow the victim to talk about the abuse when he or she wants to. They try to protect the victim from any future abuse. Such families make it easier for the victim to recover from the negative effects of sexual abuse.

Many families need assistance from professional counselors to help them recover from the problems caused by sexual abuse. This is especially true if incest was involved because relationships in families where incest has taken place are very complicated. Usually, each of the family members needs help with specific problems. The counselor can help each family member recover from the effects of incest. Even more importantly, the counselor can help the family make changes so that the sexual abuse doesn't happen again.

Chapter Five
A guide to beginning recovery

You are not responsible for the sexual abuse that
happened to you when you were a child. You *are*
responsible for the way you think, feel and act
today. You, *and only you*, can decide how you will
live the rest of your life. You, *and only you*, can
make the changes you desire. Other people can help
you achieve the things you want, but *you* must do
the work. Remember, you have some important
strengths! You have gotten yourself through some
really tough times in the past. You have the
strength and ability to make the changes you want
now!

How can a victim of child sexual abuse change the
way he or she thinks, feels and acts?

There are many things you can do to make changes.
That is what this chapter is about. You can
accomplish many of these things on your own, but
very often it is helpful to have a professional
counselor help you work on making the changes
you want.

All of the problems resulting from child sexual
abuse can be corrected even if they have gone on for
many years. Of course, the bigger the problems are
and the longer they have lasted, the more work it
will take for you to make the changes you want. If
the problems are very big and have lasted for a long
time, you will probably need a professional
counselor to help you make these changes.

If you are not able to make things better for yourself on your own, even after you have tried some of the suggestions in this chapter, consider getting help from a professional counselor. If you think of suicide frequently, the best thing you can do for yourself is to seek professional help immediately.

Even if your situation is not this extreme, it is comforting and helpful to have an understanding person to talk to about your problems. An understanding person can help you work them out in your own mind. People who do not have special training often have trouble understanding your experiences and feelings but professional counselors can. Counselors can also offer suggestions and teach you skills to help you make the changes you desire.

Getting started

Okay, you have decided that you want to change some of the ways you think, feel and act. You are reading this book to help you do this. Now, how do you begin?

The best way to begin is to attack each problem individually, one at a time. Remember the different effects of child sexual abuse that we discussed in Chapter Four. Let's start with those.

Confusion

Confusion is a big problem for many victims of child sexual abuse. They are often confused about what happened to them and why. They are also confused about their own reactions and emotions.

Learning more about child sexual abuse

One way to reduce your confusion about the things that happened to you is to learn as much as you can about child sexual abuse. Reading books like this one will help you understand more about your experiences. Many other books are available that can give you information about child sexual abuse. Look in the Additional Resources section at the end of this book for the names of some of these. Your public library can probably help you find them. You can also find much information about child sexual abuse on the Internet, including at the website for the publisher of this book:

www.cleananpress.com

You can talk with other victims of child sexual abuse to help reduce your confusion. You can read novels or see television shows about victims of child sexual abuse to learn more about the problem and its solutions. Can you think of other ways you can get more information about child sexual abuse?

Sometimes questions still remain in your mind even after learning much about sexual abuse. Then it is a good idea to ask an expert to help you find the answers. A professional counselor is most likely to be able to answer the questions you have about child sexual abuse. You can reduce much of your confusion about your own experience by learning as much as possible about child sexual abuse.

Another source of confusions for victims of child sexual abuse is not being sure exactly what happened to them when they were abused. Sometimes it is difficult for a young child to understand just what is happening when the abuse takes place. Later this makes it hard to remember exactly what did happen. Sometimes victims who do understand what is happening try to block out memories of the sexual abuse. Other times this happens without much effort.

It is important for you to have a clear picture in your mind of exactly what happened to you. This will help reduce some of the confusion you feel about your experiences.

Go over the events that took place in your own mind. Who abused you? How did the abuse start? How long did it continue? What kinds of sexual acts did the abuse involve? How did the abuse end? What happened then?

It may be very unpleasant for you to think about these things, but knowing exactly what happened is important. When you are sure of what happened, you don't feel so confused. If you have difficulty remembering just what happened, going over the events in your mind or talking about them with someone else may help you remember.

A professional counselor can probably suggest other ways to help you remember forgotten or confused events.

Understanding your feelings

Confusion about feelings is another problem for victims of child sexual abuse. You can learn to understand the feelings that many victims experience by reading Chapter Four and other books about sexual abuse such as those listed in the Additional Resources section. It is also important to identify and sort out your own feelings about many things. This will take some effort and may cause you some pain, but it will help you feel better in the long run.

Most of the time, people do not have all pleasant or unpleasant feelings about someone or something. Rather, we usually have some pleasant feelings and some unpleasant feelings about something that has happened to us or about a certain person. You can reduce your feelings of confusion if you sort out these pleasant and unpleasant feelings. So let's get started.

What unpleasant feelings do *you* have towards the person who abused *you*? Victims often feel anger and fear toward their abuser. Do you have any of these feelings? What exactly are you angry about? What exactly do you fear? What other unpleasant feelings do you have toward the person who abused you? It would be helpful for you to make a list of these feelings.

It is normal to have these unpleasant feelings. There is nothing wrong with you for having them. It is natural to have unpleasant feelings toward someone who has harmed you. But if you keep strong unpleasant feelings with you for a long time, you only harm yourself more. We will talk later about getting rid of some of these unpleasant feelings.

In addition to the unpleasant feelings, many victims of child sexual abuse also have pleasant feelings towards the person who abused them. This is especially true if the abuser was a friend or a relative. This is not unusual, but may be confusing.

It is perfectly normal to have pleasant feelings toward your abuser, in addition to the unpleasant ones. No person does *only* bad things even if he or she does *some* bad things. The abuser has probably done many good things as well as the bad things. So it is natural to have some pleasant feelings toward him or her.

Try to identify whatever pleasant feelings you have towards the person who abused you. What pleasant memories do you have of that person? What nice things did he or she do for you in addition to the harmful things?

Because of the sexual abuse you suffered, you probably have many feelings toward other people beside the abuser. Let's look at your feelings toward these other people now.

First of all, let's look at your parents. Try to identify your pleasant and unpleasant feelings toward your parents because of the sexual abuse. Many victims blame their parents for not preventing the sexual abuse or are angry at them because they did not stop the abuse from taking place. Do you feel this way? What other unpleasant feelings do you have toward each parent? Why? What pleasant feelings do you have toward each parent? Why?

Next, think about the pleasant and unpleasant feelings you have toward other family members. What unpleasant feelings do you have toward each one of them? Why do you have these feelings? What did each person do that you dislike? What pleasant feelings do you have toward each family member? What did each person in your family do to help you with the problems caused by the abuse? What other feelings do you have toward family members?

What other people outside your family were involved in the sexual abuse or its aftermath? What unpleasant feelings do you have toward specific friends and acquaintances? What unpleasant feelings do you have toward teachers, counselors, medical personnel, legal personnel or others that you came into contact with because of the sexual abuse? What did they do that you dislike? What pleasant feelings do you have toward each of these people? What did each person do that was helpful?

Finally, try to examine your pleasant and unpleasant feelings toward yourself. Let's look at the unpleasant feelings first. Did you, or do you now, blame yourself for the abuse? Are you angry at yourself in any way? Do you fear your own feelings or behaviors? Try to identify each unpleasant feeling that you have toward yourself as a result of the sexual abuse. Which one seemed strongest at first? Did any of the feelings change with time?

Perhaps some increased and some decreased. Right now, which of these unpleasant feelings seems strongest in you? In what ways do you feel worse about yourself because of the sexual abuse?

Now, let's examine the positive feelings you have about yourself because of the sexual abuse. They may be difficult to find, but you probably can discover some if you try hard enough. What things can you feel good about? Look for reasons to pat yourself on the back.

If you found a way to stop the sexual abuse, you can be proud of your ability to do this. If you told someone about the sexual abuse, you can be proud of your courage. If you were able to live through the sexual abuse, you can look at yourself as a strong person in many ways. What skills did you use to get through the experience of sexual abuse and the problems it caused?

If you are reading this book, you can feel good that you are doing something for yourself to make changes in your life. What else are you doing for yourself to make your life better? What strengths and skills are you using to do this?

So now you have started to examine your feelings. Good work! It has been hard figuring out just what feelings you have toward the people involved in your sexual abuse. You have done it—or at least you have made a start. Sometimes it takes a while to figure everything out. The more you think about it however, the clearer your feelings become and the less confused you are.

You have probably reduced some of your confusion by sorting out some of your feelings. You may have also realized that these feelings are not as frightening or as overwhelming as you thought they were. The unknown is more frightening than the known. Now you know more about your feelings. You know what they are. You know which ones you want to keep. You know which ones you want to work on changing. *You* know more about *you*!

You probably discovered you have many "mixed" feelings about people and events. Being able to recognize and live with conflicting feelings is a sign of maturity. It shows that you can accept the fact that everything in this world is not simple, not black and white. Every person is not good or bad. Each of us does some good things and some bad things. Accepting the fact that the world is not simple is part of becoming a mature adult.

Feelings are neither right nor wrong. They are the way you feel. You have a right to your feelings, whatever they are. Some feelings are helpful to you and some feelings may cause you difficulties, but do not let anyone tell you that you "should" or "should not" feel a certain way. You may want to change some of your feelings, but that is your decision.

Maybe you want to share some of the feelings you have identified in yourself. You may want other people to know and understand how you feel. Perhaps you want the abuser to know, or maybe you want your family members to know. Perhaps you want your counselor or your friends to know.

Some people will welcome knowing what your feelings are even if they are unpleasant. Other people may have difficulty accepting your feelings.

Sharing feelings with other people involves risks. Maybe others won't understand. Maybe they won't care. Maybe they will make fun of your feelings or try to use them against you. Or, maybe they will be honored that you trusted them by sharing your feelings. Maybe they will be glad to know you better.

Only you can decide which feelings you want to share and with whom you want to share them. Your counselor can help you make these decisions. Your counselor can also help you plan how to share your feelings with someone effectively—if you decide to do this.

We have talked about two ways to reduce your confusion, first, by learning more about child sexual abuse, including what happened to you, and second, by identifying and understanding your own feelings. You have probably already come a long way toward reducing your confusion if you have followed the suggestions presented in this chapter so far.

Now we will look more closely at some of the unpleasant emotions you may want to reduce in yourself: anger, fear, shame, guilt and depression.

Anger

The first step toward getting rid of your angry
feelings is to recognize the anger and admit it to
yourself. Then you can examine it.

Who are you angry at? At the abuser? At yourself?
At your parents? At the world? Are you just
annoyed, or are you furious and full of rage?

What do you do with your anger? Do you express it
or do you keep it bottled up inside. Do you tell
people about your anger? Do you do something to
change the things that make you angry, or do you
express your anger in negative ways? Do you yell at
people? Do you tease or criticize others? Do you
break things? Do you hurt yourself? What have you
done to express your anger in the past? What would
you like to do to show people how angry you are?
Do you ever secretly think about the things you
would like to do to show your anger?

There is nothing wrong with feeling anger. Anger is
a signal to us that something is wrong, that
something needs to be done! A child, or any person,
has the right to feel angry when treated badly.
Feeling anger means that you care about yourself
and believe that you should be treated better.

Using anger constructively

Many people have been taught that anger is bad. It is true that expressing anger in negative, aggressive ways can be harmful but it is possible to express anger in positive and constructive ways too. If you are being treated badly, you have the right to be angry. You have the right to do something to change the way you are being treated! You use your anger constructively when you do something to change the situation, and you reduce your angry feelings.

If you are angry about something that is going on right now, think of ways you can change the situation so that the things you dislike will stop.

If you are angry about something that happened in the past, which you cannot change, think of ways you can keep it from happening again to you or to other people in the future. What can you do to stop yourself from being victimized again? How can you help other children avoid being sexually abused? These are some of the positive ways you can use your anger to help yourself and others.

Expressing your anger

There are also positive ways you can release and reduce your anger. Sometimes it helps to write a letter to the person who abused you. You should not send the letter. It is private, just for you. It is a way for you to get some of those angry feelings out of you. Because the letter is just for you and not for the person to whom you are writing, you can even write a letter to someone who you don't know anymore or to someone who is dead.

Write all your angry thoughts in the letter. Don't hold back. Call the person all the angry names you wish. Tell the person how much he or she hurt you and how it has hurt. Pour all your anger, guilt, shame and confusion into the letter. If you have a tape recorder, you might want to dictate the letter into it instead. Yell if you feel like it!

Now read over your letter or play back your tape. Are there more angry things you want to say? Add them. Go over the letter again. Put down all the angry thoughts and feelings you have had for so long—all the things you've wished you could say!

Now, put the letter away somewhere private. Take it out and read I again several times during the next week or two. Add more to the letter until you have said everything you want to say to the person who abused you.

Now comes the time to let go of your feelings. Take out the letter you have written. Rip it to shreds! Tear it into smaller and smaller pieces. Crumple up the pieces and throw them away. Imagine that you are throwing away your angry thoughts and feelings with those ripped and crumpled pieces.

Some angry thoughts and feelings about that person will still remain but probably not as many as before. You have gotten rid of some of them.

Perhaps you are angry at other people too. Write each of them a letter as well. Like before, read it over, then rip it up and throw away the pieces.

Another positive way to express your anger is to talk about the things you are angry about. You let out some of those angry feelings when you tell another person how angry you are and why. The anger doesn't go away completely, but it is no longer trapped inside of you. You no longer feel so bad.

It is hard to talk about being angry. It is hard to show someone that you are angry if you have never allowed yourself to do this before. You may have been taught to be passive and accept whatever happens without showing any emotion, especially anger. It may feel strange to express your anger at first, but try to do it a little bit at a time.

Of course, you are taking a risk because you don't know how the other person will react. It is a risk that is worth taking. Be sure to find a caring and understanding person who is willing to listen to your anger. Find someone who won't tell you that it is wrong to feel angry. Your counselor is probably the safest person to trust with your angry feelings.

Sometimes you feel so much anger that it is hard to think about your feelings without losing control. Then vigorous physical activity can help reduce your anger to a level where you can think and talk about it without feeling like you are going to explode. Running, chopping wood, hitting a punching bag, beating a pillow, slamming doors, yelling, playing basketball, dancing wildly, chomping on crackers, swimming, anything that takes a lot of energy can help you vent your anger.

Be careful though! Sometimes other people are not very tolerant of some of these activities. You have to use your judgment in choosing a safe way to vent your anger that will work well for you. And remember, venting anger is just a temporary way to reduce pressure inside you. Feeling the need to vent anger regularly is a signal that you have not found effective ways to deal with your anger yet. You need to learn better skills to manage your anger—and you can.

Feelings of anger often lead to desires for revenge. People sometimes want to take out all the hurt they have suffered on someone else. Usually we can't hurt the person we would like to hurt, possibly the abuser, so we take it out on other people—or even ourselves. These are negative ways of expressing anger.

We usually don't feel any better after hurting someone else. We still feel anger, but now the other person feels bad as well, and we may feel guilty for our acts. So, negative ways of expressing anger are usually not useful in helping us feel better. Positive ways of expressing anger work better.

Sometimes victims are still angry many years after being sexually abused. You can still use this anger constructively, even after so long a time, to help yourself recover from the effects of the abuse. You can draw energy from your anger to make yourself take steps to change the way you think, feel and act. Making yourself talk about your anger to an understanding listener is one way to start finding better ways to change your angry feelings and improve your life.

Fear

Fear is the natural reaction to expecting that a painful experience may take place. It alerts us that we need to take some action to protect ourselves. Children do not need to feel bad for being afraid.

Children often believe there is little they can do to protect themselves, particularly from someone who is older and more powerful, like a child abuser. So they do nothing—and remain frightened.

You are no longer a child. You are no longer helpless. You can do something now to overcome your fears.

Recognizing fear

The first step toward overcoming fear is to recognize it and admit that the fear exists. Exactly what do you fear? Make a list of the fears you have now because of the sexual abuse you suffered as a child.

Look at the different fears discussed on page 58. Which of these things do you fear? Do you have a lot of fears or just a few? How strong is each one? Which things do you fear the most? Do you fear people, or places, or fear that certain things will happen?

Now look closely at your fears. Which of the fears that you have listed are realistic fears? Which are not very realistic? How can you avoid the things you fear? What can you do to handle the situation if something you fear does happen? You can reduce your fears by being prepared for these situations and knowing how you will handle them. That is what fire drills are all about.

If you are so afraid of certain people or places or things that you change your whole life around just to avoid them, these fears may be called phobias. A professional counselor can help you learn to face the things you fear and even feel comfortable with them. This may be hard to believe, but you can do it!

Sometimes when a person is very fearful, he or she has frightening dreams. Does this happen to you? Have you had any nightmares recently? What were they about? Sometimes nightmares help us recognize and overcome our fears. When you have reduced your fears, your frightening nightmares will probably stop.

Reducing anxieties

One very common fear felt by victims of child sexual abuse is the fear that some physical damage has been done to them. Do you fear this? If so, a thorough physical examination would answer your questions. Any medical problems the physician finds could then be treated properly. However, most victims of child sexual abuse have no physical problems. You can relieve your mind of worry by finding out that you have suffered no physical damage because of the abuse.

If you have gotten to the point where you are fearful much of the time, but you don't know exactly what you fear, this is called anxiety. There are many ways to control anxiety. It is most helpful to have a professional counselor assist you with this, however.

Sometimes just identifying the things you have feared in the past and the things you fear right now will help you reduce your anxiety. This is especially true if you can take steps to make sure that the things you fear don't happen or that you can handle them when they do happen.

Sometimes when we really look at the things we fear, they turn out not to be so fearful after all. Many times things that are extremely frightening to children are not so fearful to adults. If we become frightened of something as a child and never stop to examine our fear, we may carry that fear into adulthood. Then we feel just as frightened as we did when we were children, but without good reason. As an adult, we can often look at the thing we feared and decide it is not so fearful after all.

Okay, you have identified your fears and you have looked at each one closely. Now what are *you* going to do about each one?

Which ones are not so frightening as you thought earlier? Which ones are you just going to "live with?" Which ones are you going to work on reducing? How are you going to do this?

If you are not sure how to start reducing your fears, a professional counselor can help. Who are you going to get to help you work on reducing your fears?

Shame

Many people who were victims of child sexual abuse feel dirty or shameful as a result. They feel different from other people. It can help to know that this is not true. You are not so different. Many other people have had similar experiences.

You are not alone

The stories of other victims in Chapter Three can show you that you are not alone. The information about statistics in Chapter One also tells you the same story. Let's see what those statistics that say "at least 25% of adults were victims of child sexual abuse" really mean.

The next time you are in a group of people—at the movies, at church, in the grocery store—look around you. One out of every four people you see was also a victim of child sexual abuse!

Count the number of people in the theater the next time you go to see a movie. If there are 200 people there, at least 50 of them probably were, or are, victims of child sexual abuse! Fifty people right there in the theater with you! That is a lot of people. You aren't so different after all.

Can you tell which ones of those 200 people are the 50 who were abused? Look at the people sitting in your row. If there are ten people in your row, at least one of them, other than you, was probably a victim too! Which person is it? Can you tell? Do you think he or she can pick you out as having been a victim too?

Of course this is silly. No one can identify victims of child sexual abuse just by looking at them. If they could, then it would be a lot easier to stop the sexual abuse of children!

Still, you may *feel* different. You may feel dirty and shameful. You may believe that if people knew about the sexual abuse, they would not like you.

Understanding others

That is probably true of some people. There are some people in this world who won't like you because you are too skinny or too fat or too loud or too quiet or too smart or too silly or too old or too young. There are people who won't like you because

88

of your skin color or because you chew gum or because you come from a different neighborhood or because you were sexually abused.

People have various reasons for not liking you if they know you were sexually abused. Some may not know much about sexual abuse. They may wrongly think that the abuse was your fault, so they may not like you.

Others may be afraid of sexual abuse happening to them or to someone they love and be unable to face their own fears. Seeing you may bring those fears to mind, so they avoid you.

Some people may think that because you were sexually abused you know a lot about sex, perhaps more than you should. They may think of you as strange or different for that reason and may not like you. There can be other reasons as well.

So, yes, some people who find out that you were sexually abused may not like you because of it, but as you know, not everyone would like you anyway— even if you hadn't been sexually abused.

People who are understanding and caring will know that you, as the victim, have suffered because of what the abuser did. They know that you, the victim, did not deserve to suffer. They will like you or dislike you because of the person you are and the way you behave, not because of what happened to you.

You do not need to feel ashamed for being a victim of child sexual abuse. There is nothing wrong or bad about you because of it. As you learn more about this problem, you will realize that you do not need to feel shame for having been a victim. Talking with other victims of child sexual abuse can also help you realize that they, and you, are not different from other people and need not feel shame

Guilt

The victims of child sexual abuse often wonder, "Why me? Why did this happen to me and not someone else?" or "What did I do that was so terribly wrong to deserve having something like this happen to me?"

It was not the child's fault that he or she was chosen to be the victim of sexual abuse. The child is not responsible for the abuse. The child happened to be available when the abuser needed to fulfill his or her own needs.

The most important thing for you, the victim, to remember is that *total* responsibility for the abuse lies with the *abuser*. This is even true if you enjoyed some of what happened. This is true even if the abuser says the abuse was your fault. This is true even if you received special rewards because of the abuse. This is true even if you did not try hard enough to make the abuse stop.

It is not your fault

It was not your fault if someone tricked, trapped, bribed or forced you into sexual contact. If someone touches a child in a sexual way and the child does not stop the contact for whatever reason, it is not the child's fault.

Most children assume they are guilty for being sexually abused. When the sexual abuse is discovered, it often causes a crisis in the family. Most children then assume that this crisis is also their fault and feel guilty for the crisis too. They think, "I must have done something terribly wrong." Again, this is not true. Total responsibility for the abuse and for any crisis that results lies with the abuser.

The person who sexually abuses a child has serious psychological problems and needs help. The child was the victim of the abuser's problems. The abuser *chose* to harm the child to meet his or her own needs.

Abusers are usually older and more powerful than their child victims. The child has the right to expect protection, not abuse, from the abuser. When a child is abused, he or she has the right to tell others about the sexual abuse. The abuser, not the child, must assume full responsibility for any disruption that takes place because the sexual abuse was reported.

Do you feel guilty in any way about the sexual abuse you suffered or about anything that happened afterwards? Do you have feelings that the sexual abuse was your fault? Do you feel guilty for any of the things you did to stop the abuse? Do you feel guilty for any of the things that happened to your family or to the abuser? For exactly which things do you feel guilty?

Feeling guilty doesn't make it true

Just because you *feel* guilty doesn't make it true! You can change the way you feel by changing the things you tell yourself. If you tell yourself that the sexual abuse was your fault, then of course, you will feel bad. So stop telling yourself something that isn't true, something that is inaccurate!

The sexual abuse was not your fault. You know that now. Keep pointing this out to yourself whenever you notice feelings of guilt. Argue with yourself! Once you truly accept the fact that you were the victim and not the person responsible for the abuse, you can stop feeling guilty about being abused.

Sometimes a child who is being sexually abused takes advantage of the sexual abuse in some way. He or she may use the abuse to gain special privileges or to take advantage of other family members. If you did this and feel guilty about it, perhaps you have a good reason for this feeling. You feel guilty because you used other people in a bad way. But even if you did make some mistakes, there is no reason to keep punishing yourself, even in your own mind, for mistakes you made or bad things you did. You can forgive yourself for your mistakes. Let them be a lesson to you and a guide to better behavior in the future.

Make sure you sort out which things you really might have been responsible for, like taking advantage of others, and which things were the responsibility of the abuser or of someone else.

Depression and suicide

Victims of child sexual abuse often become depressed. Many victims live with a low level of depression for years. Even though things never get so bad that they cannot function, life seems to hold little joy for them. Other victims become even more depressed so that they have trouble functioning at all in everyday life.

Seeking help

When you are depressed, it is hard to believe that your situation can improve. Depression makes people view themselves, the world and the future in a very negative way. This view is not accurate even though it *seems* accurate to the depressed person.

If you are depressed, a professional counselor can help you pull yourself out of this unhappy state. The treatment of depression is highly specialized and cannot be discussed in detail here. Professional counselors know a lot about various ways of treating depression, and treatment is usually successful. If you are depressed, a professional counselor can help you. Seek one out.

Sometimes victims of child sexual abuse become so depressed that suicide seems like the only escape from unhappiness. Unfortunately, suicide is a permanent solution to what often turns out to be a temporary problem.

Seeking alternatives

People kill themselves when they see no other alternatives. Yet there are usually many alternatives, some of which have good consequences and some bad. If you are seriously considering suicide, talk with a professional counselor who can help you find those better alternatives. Most people who attempt suicide and fail are later very glad that they failed. They often go on to find more ways of living happier lives than they ever imagined possible.

Suicide always remains as a final alternative. You owe it to yourself to try out other alternatives first. You can always kill yourself later, but you cannot try other, and possibly better, alternatives once you have ended your life.

In many ways, you are a very strong person if you have survived child sexual abuse. You have gotten yourself through some very bad times.

If you are considering suicide, think about that. You could have chosen to die earlier in your life, but you chose to keep living. You can continue to choose to live. You can make your life much better than it is now. Reading this book is one of the things you are already doing to make your life better. What else can you do to improve your life?

Self-esteem

Self-esteem means liking yourself. It means being able to say, "I'm okay," and meaning it. It means believing "I am an important, worthwhile person just because I am me."

Being treated badly by the abuser may have convinced you that you are worthless and that no one could ever love or care about you. This is not true. Each person in this world has some good qualities and some bad qualities. Each of us is important. Each of us is worthwhile. Each of us can be loved and cherished by many others and by ourselves.

This is hard to believe sometimes. Even people who have not been sexually abused worry about not being loved or cared for, or about being worthwhile.

You are important

There are many ways to learn to believe that you are important. First of all, you must be open to accepting the possibility that you are worthwhile and capable of being loved.

If you find yourself continuing to be a victim of physical abuse, sexual abuse, or being "used" or hurt by other people, poor self-esteem may be the problem. You can do something to change this.

Stop for a minute and examine your own beliefs about yourself. Certainly you have some "bad points"—unless you are the most perfect person who ever lived!—but probably not as many bad points as you have been telling yourself.

First of all, identify all the negative thoughts, feelings and beliefs you have about yourself. Are there a lot of them? Even though these seem accurate to you, this is probably not the way you appear to other people. Perhaps your ideas are a little distorted.

Recognizing your good traits

Everybody has some bad traits, but each person also has good traits. Probably part of you believes that you have some good qualities too. Listen to that part of you.

Now make a list of your good qualities, your strong points, the things about yourself that you admire. These might include caring, creativity, intelligence, special talents, good health, understanding, strength, a nice smile, what else? Count even the little things. They are important too.

There are a lot more good qualities than you thought, aren't there? Once you start looking for them and identifying your good qualities, you start increasing your self-esteem.

You may be surprised to know that most victims of child sexual abuse tell themselves very bad things about themselves. They only look at their negative qualities. So if you have been doing this, your reaction is a common one.

Know also that, just like everyone else, you have good qualities and strengths as well. There is no reason to deny the bad features in your personality, but there is no reason to deny all the good ones either. Now remember, with all your good qualities and bad qualities, you are an important, worthwhile person. You are someone worth caring about!

Helping others

One way to increase your self-esteem is by recognizing your good qualities as well as your bad qualities. Another way to increase your self-esteem is by doing things to help other people.

You may believe that you need so much help yourself, you could never help other people. This is not true. Even though everything is not perfect for you, you can still be a great help to others in many ways. Smiling at another person or paying someone a genuine compliment can do wonders to help them feel good about themselves.

Notice the people around you. What little things can you do that will help them feel better about themselves? Try it. Don't you feel better about yourself knowing you have brightened someone else's day, even just a little bit? Think of the power you have!

Setting goals

A third way to increase your self-esteem is to see yourself making progress towards your own goals. In order to do this, you must first *have* some goals. Exactly what are your goals? What would you like to have accomplished one year from now? One month from now? By tomorrow?

How will you go about reaching you goals? What are you doing right now to work toward each goal?

It is helpful to write down your goals for the day, week, month, year, and even longer. Then write down the small steps it will take to reach each goal so that as you complete each step you can check it off. That way you can recognize the progress you are making toward the goals you want to reach.

Accomplishments of any kind, however small, can help you realize that you are a capable and important person. Remember to pat yourself on the back for each small accomplishment you make and for each small goal you reach.

Sometimes people are afraid to say nice things to themselves or to give themselves credit for their accomplishments or for their good qualities. They are afraid that this means they are conceited or a "show-off." This is not true.

Each person needs to feel good about him or herself. Being a good friend to yourself means accepting your strengths and accomplishments as well as your weaknesses and mistakes.

Many times no one will notice your accomplishments except you. If no one else is patting you on the back for them, you need to do this for yourself. Don't be afraid to try it. Be lavish with your praise of yourself. After all, each accomplishment was something you worked to achieve. You deserve your praise for that.

One important goal you may want to work toward is preventing sexual abuse from happening to other children. Things you can do to achieve this include working to

- Make the public more aware of the problem of child sexual abuse.

- Protect your own children from sexually abusive situations.

- Teach your own children how to avoid becoming victims of child sexual abuse. Look in the Additional Resources section for books that can help you do this.

- Encourage parents and schools to teach children how to avoid sexual abuse.

- Encourage the reporting of child sexual abuse to the authorities.

- Encourage the enforcement of laws protecting children from child sexual abuse.

- Encourage support of treatment programs for victims of sexual abuse *and* for sexual abusers.

Finally, you can increase your self-esteem greatly as you work toward overcoming the effects of having been a victim of child sexual abuse. As you are learning in this book, there are many things you can do to work towards these goals. Don't forget to pat yourself on the back as you see yourself making changes in your life.

Trusting

Many victims of child sexual abuse have trouble trusting people again. This is especially true for those abused in continuing relationships or incest. This is understandable because these victims were hurt by someone they trusted.

Sometimes it takes a very long time to allow yourself to trust others again. Trusting someone is always taking a risk. Sometimes the trust you place in another person will be rewarded but other times it will be betrayed. It is painful to trust someone and then be hurt by that person. This is true for anyone, not only victims of child sexual abuse.

Going through life without trusting anyone is very lonely however. So, even though it is risky, at times each of us wants to place our trust in someone. Because one or two people betray our trust does not mean that everyone will. If we look carefully, we can find people who are worthy of our trust.

Consider yourself for example. Are you trustworthy? Can other people trust you? If you know you can be trusted, then there must be other people out there like you who can also be trusted.

Do you find yourself suspicious of the motives of everyone? Are there some people that you allow yourself to trust, at least a little? Who have you trusted correctly in the past? Who is the person you trust the most right now?

The more you allow yourself to trust someone and find that trust rewarded, the more willing you will be to trust other people in the future. You have to take a chance to learn to trust. Like any other risky operation, you want to go slowly.

Social skills

Victims of incest often find that they do not know how to get along well with people their own age. They have had little chance to be with others while growing up. They may feel uncomfortable and lacking in social skills.

They may not know how to talk easily to other people or how to make friends. They may find that they don't share the same interests as their schoolmates, especially if they have had to take on many responsibilities around the house.

Sometimes they start acting older than their age. Other times they behave only in sexual ways towards others because this is the only way they know how to behave.

Sometimes victims of other types of child sexual abuse also lack social skills. They may have begun avoiding people after the abuse because they felt "different" and so they did not learn how to get along easily with other people as they grew older.

Some victims of child sexual abuse may have felt uncomfortable around other people even before the abuse. Abusers find it easier to make victims of children who already feel unsure of themselves.

Whatever the reason may be that you do not feel comfortable with other people, there are things you can do to make changes in yourself now.

Learning to get along easily with other people is just like learning any other skill. It takes practice. You get better at it gradually. It doesn't happen overnight or by magic. It takes some work. You make some mistakes while you are learning.

There are many self-help books written about social skills and getting along with other people. Some of these might be helpful to you if you believe this is a problem for you.

Forcing yourself to start participating in social activities even if you are shy or unsure of yourself is one way to gain practice in these areas. It is hard to make yourself participate sometimes, but it becomes easier the more you do.

Talking with others about the way they see you is something you can do to identify your own behaviors that cause problems with other people. Talking with a counselor about these behaviors can also be useful.

102

Relationships

Later relationships are often difficult for the victims of child sexual abuse. It is hard for girls who have been sexually abused to trust boys or men. Sometimes the only way girls know how to relate to a male is sexually. They may be overly seductive which can lead to further abuse. They may be so frightened of men that they avoid all contact with them, which cuts them off from normal social relationships and fun. The same thing can happen to sexually abused boys.

Sometimes victims of child sexual abuse become involved in a series of promiscuous sexual relationships to prove that they are desirable, worthwhile and that there is nothing wrong with them. Eventually, this hurts them and further reduces their self-esteem.

The healthiest thing you can do is go slowly in your new relationships. You need time to build up your self-confidence and your trust in other people.

Think about the kinds of relationships you want. Are you developing these relationships now? What can you do to find the kind of relationships you want?

Sometimes women who were victims of child sexual abuse choose mates who abuse them or their children. One thing you can do to avoid this is to work on increasing your own self-esteem. Another thing you can do is to think very carefully about any potential mate. Are there indications that he might treat you or your children badly?

You do not have to accept an abusive mate. An abusive mate is *not* better than no one. You have the potential to make a life for yourself, by yourself. You also have the potential to find someone who will truly love you and treat you well.

If you work on developing your skills, your self-confidence and your self-esteem, you will find that you can come to depend on *yourself* to take care of *you*. You can make it just fine on your own—even though it takes some work, planning, problem-solving and even some mistakes along the way.

Once you realize that you are a capable, worthwhile, independent person, you can choose to be with a partner if you want. You won't feel forced into bad relationships because you have "no choice."

If you are living with someone who is mistreating you or your children, it is your responsibility to do something to stop the abuse. This may be difficult to do, but you are responsible for protecting your children. If you have difficulty doing this, there are many agencies that can provide you with support and counseling. You must take the first step of contacting them.

Attitudes toward sex

Many victims of child sexual abuse have come to believe that sex is dirty, shameful or fearful. Such a belief can cause you difficulties in relationships and in sexual adjustment. This belief is wrong.

Sex can be a wonderfully enjoyable activity. It can bring you much pleasure and happiness. Sex itself is not wrong. The way you were involved in a sexual relationship was what was wrong. Sex that is tricked, trapped, forced or bribed cannot be beneficial to the victim. Sex within a loving, caring relationship can be one of the greatest joys in life.

Going slowly in developing sexual relationships is important. You will enjoy sex and come to feel more comfortable about it if you have a loving, trusting relationship with your partner before your sexual relationship begins.

If you still have serious sexual difficulties, even within a loving, trusting relationship, it is time to talk to a professional counselor. Most sexual problems can be treated very successfully. You should not continue to be robbed of one of life's greatest joys by the person who sexually abused you. You can do something to change this part of your life now.

Independence and Maturity

Victims of child sexual abuse often have been convinced that they have no power or control over their environment or over themselves. This is not true.

It is hard to learn to be responsible for yourself and to behave in an independent and mature way if you have not had the chance to make decisions for yourself. It is difficult to learn to take responsibility for your own actions when you never realized you had the power to make choices before.

In learning to be independent and mature, you will make some good choices and some bad choices. You are human; therefore, you will make mistakes. "Good judgment comes from experience ... and experience comes from bad judgment."

You need not "beat yourself over the head" for the mistakes you make. If you can view your mistakes as "lessons," you will learn and gain strength from them as you continue to grow.

So even though you were a victim of child sexual abuse in the past, you must learn to take responsibility for your behavior now. You have the right and the responsibility to make choices about how you will lead your life. You, and only you, can take responsibility for these choices.

If you find yourself continuing to make bad choices, a professional counselor can help you get back on the right track.

Parenting skills

If you were the victim of incest, you probably have a very poor idea of what being a good parent involves. Your own parents did not give you a good picture of the way parents should behave. This may be true for victims of other types of sexual abuse as well.

How do you learn to be a good parent if you have no one to model yourself after? Many good books are written on how to be a successful parent. You can learn parenting skills by reading some of these books.

Parenting classes are often available to new parents through hospitals, physicians or public health departments. You can talk with friends, relatives, neighbors, teachers, counselors, pediatricians, ministers or others about how to care for your children in proper ways, both physically and psychologically.

If you sincerely want to become a good parent, you will find ways to learn the skills you did not learn while growing up. You need to recognize that you may have a lot to learn in this area. Still, you are capable of learning to be a good parent.

Physical abuse of your own children

At times, parents who were victims of child sexual abuse find themselves coming close to abusing their own children physically. This is a fairly rare problem. Most victims of child sexual abuse do not abuse their children, but it does happen.

A former victim of child sexual abuse who still feels much anger, resentment and frustration because of that experience may take out these feelings on his or her own child through yelling, hitting or other abuse. A former victim who has few parenting skills may have great difficulty handling his or her children. This leads to frustration, which can also lead to abuse.

107

If you find yourself at such a point, there are many things you can do. You can seek professional counseling to help you overcome the feelings you have about your own experiences as a victim. You can take parenting classes or read books on parenting, which will help you more effectively handle the everyday problems children present so that they don't "set you off" so easily.

You can also seek assistance from a professional counselor to help you prevent or stop your physical abuse of your children. You should be aware however, that most states require counselors to report any suspected child abuse to the authorities. Child abuse is a crime, but authorities usually are more interested in preventing future abuse than in punishing past abuse.

Another thing you can do is ask for assistance from local social services agencies. Many child welfare departments offer counseling, training and other assistance to parents who want to stop abusing their children. Such parents are usually not prosecuted if they are actively involved in treatment.

The national organization, Parents Anonymous, is dedicated to helping parents who have abused their children. This organization is patterned after Alcoholics Anonymous. It provides support and encouragement to help parents stop abusing their children and to keep them from doing it in the future. You might find a local chapter listed in your telephone book.

If you abuse your children, help is available. Most parents who abuse their children also love them and feel very bad for hurting them. If you abuse your children, it is your responsibility to do something to change your behavior now. You will feel better about yourself as you take steps to change your behavior.

Sexual abuse of children

Most people who were victims of child sexual abuse do not go on to sexually abuse other children. However, some do. Most people who do sexually abuse children were themselves victims of child sexual abuse. This is a very serious problem. It is one that definitely requires professional assistance to overcome.

If you recognize tendencies toward sexual abuse in yourself, the best thing you can do for yourself, and for others, is to seek professional help immediately.

Treatment for these problems is difficult and requires much effort on your part, but it can be successful. Only *you* can prevent another child from suffering the pain you experienced as a victim of child sexual abuse.

Choosing a professional counselor

Seeking help from a professional counselor has been suggested many times in this book. Most people have never talked to a counselor before. They don't know how to find one or how to choose a good one, and choosing a good counselor who can help you solve your problems is very important, because you are important. The following information should help you find a useful counselor.

There are many types of professional counselors. These may be social workers, psychologists, ministers, psychiatrists, family counselors, mental health workers or other such people. The title that a counselor uses is not as important as the training and experience he or she has had. Experience in working with victims of child sexual abuse is especially important.

Many public agencies can recommend or provide counselors for you. Mental health centers and other public agencies usually provide free services or charge a fee based on your ability to pay.

Your local mental health center can probably give you information about its own services and about other professional counselors available in your area. The mental health center's number can be found in the Yellow Pages in the telephone book under "Mental Health Services" or "Counseling."

Before deciding on a counselor, feel free to ask about that person's education, state certification and experience working with other victims of child sexual abuse. If you were hiring a piano teacher or a plumber you would ask questions first. The same is true when you hire a professional counselor to help you.

Just because someone is a professional counselor and has helped others doesn't mean that he or she will be able to help *you*. After you have seen the counselor once or twice, you must decide for yourself whether this is the person to help *you* solve *your* problems. If you decide that this person cannot help you, you have the right to look for someone else who can.

One way to decide if this person will be able to help you in solving your problems is to ask yourself some questions.

- Do I feel comfortable with this counselor?

- Is this counselor willing to tell me how he or she plans to help me?

- Does this counselor say things that make sense?

- Does this counselor seem genuinely interested in me and my life?

- Does this counselor act like a consultant who is working for me, or does this counselor try to run my life?

- Does this counselor seem interested in helping me make the changes in my life that I want, or does this counselor tell me what changes I should make?

- Is this counselor willing to discuss the sexual abuse I suffered, or does he or she say, "Forget the past"?

- In general, after talking with this counselor, do I feel more hopeful, or do I usually feel worse about myself?

Remember, you have the right to keep looking for a counselor who will help you until you find the right one. You have the right to expect good treatment and helpful results!

The counselor works for you. If you don't like the job he or she is doing, fire this counselor and find someone who will do a better job. Demand a competent, helpful counselor. You have the right to demand! You are an important, worthwhile person!

Keep in mind though, that you cannot expect your counselor to magically "fix" whatever is wrong. Your counselor will help you figure out how to make the changes you want in your life. Your counselor cannot make those changes for you. You must do the work yourself.

Unfortunately, some unethical counselors do exist. Victims of child sexual abuse are especially vulnerable to further sexual abuse. If your counselor suggests any type of sexual contact between you and him or herself for *any* reason, this is sexual abuse. Your counselor is trying to use you to meet his or her own needs. Refuse to become a victim again! Report him or her to the professional organization and state licensing board immediately. This is malpractice in any counseling profession— no matter what your counselor says. Find a new counselor immediately.

Confidentiality

When you discuss your life with a professional counselor, the things you discuss are usually confidential. This means the counselor will not tell them to anyone else without your permission. Confidentiality is so important that the federal government and many states have passed special laws to protect your confidential information.

Sometimes there are exceptions to rules about confidentiality, however, and the counselor may be forced to tell others what you talk about. Therefore, before you talk with a counselor, it is a good idea to ask him or her exactly what kinds of things will be confidential and what will not be confidential.

Final word

You were once a victim of child sexual abuse. In some ways this has made you stronger. In other ways it has made life more difficult for you. This book has discussed a number of things you can do to recover from the negative effects of child sexual abuse. It has helped you start on your journey.

Now it is up to you to make the changes in your life that you desire. You may do this on your own, or you may seek the help of a professional counselor. You *can* change the way you think, feel and act.

You are no longer a powerless victim. You have the ability to make your own choices. You can, and must, decide how you will live the rest of your life.

May your choices bring you happiness!

Do YOU like the way you feel
after reading this book?

If ***Why Me? Help for Victims
of Child Sexual Abuse
(Even if they are adults now)***

has helped YOU,
think about other people
who could benefit from this experience.

Share this book
with one of them today,

or order copies
for all of them using the
Order Form
at the end of this book.

Help others start changing their lives today.

Additional Resources

The Internet

You can find almost anything on the Web—good or bad. Just remember that *anyone* can put *anything* on the Web. Always evaluate the information and the source carefully. Protect yourself from becoming a victim again.

Organizations

Using your search engine and appropriate keywords you can find organizations for child sexual abuse survivors of various types, for parents, for partners, for former abusers, and for treating professionals. You can find organizations devoted to preventing child sexual abuse and to educating people about it, as well as organizations supporting treatment and advocacy for child sexual abuse victims. You can also find all types of magazines, newsletters, newslists, chat groups, blogs, and whatever other ways of sharing information is currently popular for victims of child sexual abuse.

Professional Counselors

You can find Yellow Pages listings online in any town or city for counseling centers, rape crisis services, suicide hotlines, clinics, or individual professional counselors. You can also use your search engine to find websites for individual professional counselors in specific locations. These websites often tell you something about the counselor and the types of services offered, as well as fees, hours, insurance, and the location of offices.

Libraries

Many libraries have placed their catalogues online so you can look through them to find a particular book or to see what books that library has on child sexual abuse.

Online Booksellers

At websites like www.amazon.com, www.barnesanddnoble.com, and many others you can find books about child sexual abuse. Type "child sexual abuse" or other keywords, a title, or an author into the website search box. A book's table of contents and reviews, as well as lists of similar books, and even excerpts from the book are often available at each book listing. Online bookseller websites are also excellent places to read about newly published books or to purchase out-of-print books in the "Used" section.

www.cleananpress.com

Visit our website for additional information about child sexual abuse, further guidance for healing and recovery, and an opportunity to express your own opinions or to seek additional answers to your questions about child sexual abuse. We welcome your participation!

Books About Child Sexual Abuse

Look for these books at your public library, or purchase them from your online bookseller or your local bookstore. Find out more about these and other resources at our website:

www.cleananpress.com

This listing of books is not an endorsement of any of them or of the information they contain. You should learn as much as possible about child sexual abuse for yourself, but always examine information critically and tailor it to your own individual needs.

Books about the effects of child sexual abuse and its treatment

Written for professionals

- *A Sourcebook on Child Sexual Abuse*, by David Finkelhor, Sage Publications, Newbury Park, CA, 1986.

- *Handbook of Clinical Intervention in Child Sexual Abuse*, by Suzanne M. Sgroi, Lexington Books, D.C. Heath and Company, Lexington, MA, 1982.

- *Treatment of Adult Survivors of Childhood Abuse*, by Eliana Gil, Launch Press, Walnut Creek, CA, 1988.

- *Treating Sexually Abused Children and Their Families*, by Beverly James and Maria Nasjleti, Consulting Psychologists Press, Palo Alto, CA, 1983.

Written for the general public

- *The Silent Children*, by Linda T. Sanford, McGraw-Hill Book Company, New York, 1985.

- *Betrayal of Innocence: Incest and Its Devastation*, by Susan Forward and Craig Buck, Penguin Books, East Rutherford, NJ, 1988.

Books that explain the psychology of sexual abusers

- *Men Who Rape*, by Nicholas Groth with H. Jean Birnbaum, Perseus Publishing, Cambridge, Ma, 2001.

- *Unspeakable Acts: Why Men Sexually Abuse Children*, by Douglas W. Pryor, New York University Press, New York, 1999.

- *Female Sex Offenders*, by Julia Hislop, Issues Press, Enumclaw, WA, 2001.

- *Conversations with a Pedophile*, by Amy Hammel-Zabin, Barricade Books, Ft. Lee, NJ, 2003.

- *Predators: Pedophiles, Rapists, and Other Sex Offenders*, by Anna C. Salter, Basic Books, New York, 2003.

Books that tell you how to keep your children safe from child sexual abuse

Written for adults

- *No More Secrets*, by Caren Adams and Jennifer Fay, Impact Publishers, San Luis Obispo, CA, 1981.

- *Identifying Child Molesters*, by Carla Van Dorn, Haworth Press, Binghamton, NY, 2001.

Written for adults to share with children

- *No-No the Little Seal*, by Judith Feldman, Random House Books, New York, 1986.

- *My Body Is Private*, by Linda W. Girard and Kathleen Tucker, Albert Whitman & Company, Morton Grove, IL, 1984.

- *It's My Body*, by Lori Freeman, Parenting Press, Seattle, WA, 1984.

- *The Right Touch*, by Sandy Kleven and Jody Bergsma, Illumination Arts Publishing Company, Bellevue, WA, 1998.

- *Your Body Belongs to You*, by Cornelia Spelman, Albert Whitman & Company, Morton Grove, IL, 2000.

- *Top Secret: Sexual Assault Information for Teenagers Only*, by Jennifer J. Fay and Billie J. Flerchinger, King County Sexual Assault Resource Center, Renton, WA, 1982.

Books that guide recovery from child sexual abuse

Written for victims

- *It Happened to Me: A Teen's Guide to Overcoming Sexual Abuse*, by William L. Carter, New Harbinger Publications, Belton, TX, 2002.

- *The Courage to Heal: A Guide for Women Survivors of Child Sexual Abuse*, by Ellen Bass and Laura Davis, Harper-Collins, New York, 1994.

- *Victims No Longer: The Classic Guide for Men Recovering from Sexual Child Abuse, Second Edition*, by Mike Lew, Harper-Collins Publishers, New York, 2004.

Written for parents

- *Helping Your Child Recover from Sexual Abuse*, by Caren Adams, Jennifer Fay, and A.G. Fawkes, University of Washington Press, Seattle, WA, 1992.

- *When Your Child Has Been Molested*, by Kathryn Brohl and Joyce C. Potter, Josey-Boss, San Francisco, CA, 2004.

Written for partners

- *Allies in Healing*, by Laura Davis, Harper-Collins Publishers, New York, 1991.

- *What About Me? A Guide for Men Helping Female Partners Deal with Childhood Sexual Abuse*, by Grant Cameron, Creative Bound, Ottawa, ON, 1994.

Self-help guides to changing your thoughts, feelings, and behavior

- *Feeling Good*, by David D. Burns, New American Library, New York, 1980.

- *I Can If I Want To*, by Arnold Lazarus and Allen Fay, FMC Books, 2000.

- *Your Erroneous Zones*, by Wayne W. Dyer, Avon Books, New York, 1995.

- *The Relaxation and Stress Reduction Workbook*, by Martha Davis, et al., New Harbinger Publications, Oakland, CA, 2000.

- *Your Perfect Right: Assertiveness and Equality in Your Life and Relationships*, by Robert E. Alberti, Impact Publishers, Atascadero, CA, 2001.

- *What You Can Change and What You Can't*, by Martin E. Seligman, Ballantine Books, New York, 1995.

Fiction and biography with themes of child sexual abuse

Written for children or teens

- *I Can't Talk About It*, by Doris Sanford, Multnomah Publications, 1986.

- *Silver*, by Norma Fox Mazer, Harper-Collins Publishers, New York, 1988.

- *The Tale of One Bad Rat*, by Bryan Talbot, Dark Horse Comics, Milwaukee, OR, 1997.

Written for adults

- *I Know Why the Caged Bird Sings*, by Maya Angelou, Bantam, New York, 1983.

- *The Color Purple*, by Alice Walker, Washington Square Press, New York, 1998.

- *The Prince of Tides*, by Pat Conroy, Houghton Mifflin Company, New York, 1986.

About the Author

Dr. Lynn Daugherty is a psychologist actively involved in the treatment of children, adolescents and adults who were victims of child sexual abuse. She practices clinical and forensic psychology in New Mexico, where she lives with her husband, an attorney. In her current private practice and previous positions as a forensic psychologist in Montana and director of a New Mexico forensic evaluation team, she has worked extensively with both victims of sexual abuse and sex offenders for over twenty-five years. Dr. Daugherty wrote *Why Me? Help for Victims of Child Sexual Abuse (Even if they are adults now)* to make basic information about child sexual abuse and about recovery from its impact easily available to the increasing numbers of victims seeking help.

Order Form

For copies of ***Why Me? Help for Victims of Child Sexual Abuse (Even if they are adults now)*** enclose:

$15.95 for each book (includes shipping & handling)
   x ____ Number of books
     TOTAL

Send check or money order in U.S. dollars with this form to:

> Cleanan Press, Inc.
> 200 West First Street, Suite 323
> Roswell, NM 88203

(Please print clearly. This is your shipping label. We ship to U.S. addresses only.)

SHIP TO: Name_____

                  Address_____

                  _____

Email _____
      (We will never sell your information to anyone. We *will* send you
      occasional updates about our books.)

You may return this book at any time within one year of purchase for a full refund for any reason. This price is subject to change. Please consult www.cleananpress.com for current pricing. Information about discounts for larger orders is also available at this website. All books ordered with this order form are signed by the author.

Remember! You can also buy *Why Me? Help for Victims of Child Sexual Abuse (Even if they are adults now)* at Amazon.com **and other on-line booksellers, as well as from your local bookstore.**

CPSIA information can be obtained
at www.ICGtesting.com
Printed in the USA
LVHW010943260420
654460LV00003B/865